Prais

The Courage to C... .... right now, to calm our fears, answer our questions, and introduce us to the magic and mystery of the transitioning of our bodies. Filled with so many morsels, you'll want to savor them over and over again.

> ~ Leslie Bridger, Lover of Life, Author, Speaker,
> Wellness Guide & Hugger Extraordinaire

With joy and reassurance, *The Courage to Care* helps us realize that everything we need to be at someone's bedside is within ourselves—including our song. We simply need to be there.

> ~ Lana Noel, Chair, Threshold Choir Board of Directors

The Courage to Care masterfully moves us in gentle transformation from living fully to dying gracefully. Do yourself and your loved ones a favor—grab this book now, and live a better rest of your life!

> ~ Rev. Gary Nobuo Niki, Author, *d.i.y. zen and the Art
> of Gentle Emotional Transformation*

We are all those people seeking strength in the presence of the dying. Linda makes that strength attainable. Not only is *The Courage to Care* a must-read, but this book is also a must-live.

> ~ Helen Bauer, RN BSN CHPN,
> Co-owner The Heart of Hospice, LLC, and
> Co-host of The Heart of Hospice Podcast

Linda takes us from the big picture of dying–its challenges and opportunities–to the specific and practical information that many people will find helpful. Her use of storytelling is particularly effective at bringing her understandings and wisdom to life.

~ Janet Booth, End-of-Life RN, Educator, Author, *Re-Imagining the End of Life: Self-Development and Reflective Practices for Nurse Coaches*

Full of wise counsel and stories that will land in the mind of your heart and stay there as guidance and reminders of what is possible...a work of love and truth...for each of us to approach death with confidence and sensitivity.

~ Kathy Leo, Founder, Hallowell Hospice Choir, and Author, *On the Breath of Song: The Practice of Bedside Singing for the Dying*

Kudos to Linda Bryce! While heart-wrenching for us, can there be a more important time to be fully present than when a loved one passes? With love and understanding, Linda gives us the *Courage to Care.*

~ Kevin Conklin - Life Coach & Spiritual Guide

A brilliant resource BEFORE a loved one's death is imminent, AND a healing read even after losing someone.

~ Rosie Guagliardo, InnerBrilliance Coaching

From personal experience, I know that every moment with a loved one through their dying is ineffable and unforgettable. Linda's work is a rare gift of loving, seasoned guidance we all need for this profoundly sacred and tender time of togetherness.

~ Jamie Leno Zimron, The Centered Way / Psychologist, Aikido Sensei, LPGA Pro

The Courage to Care

Being Fully Present with the Dying

LINDA BRYCE

Capucia Publishing
York, Pennsylvania

Paperback ISBN: 978-1-954920-04-0
eBook ISBN: 978-1-954920-05-7
Library of Congress Control Number: 2021905108

Cover Design: Ranilo Cabo
Layout: Ranilo Cabo
Editor and Proofreader: Janis Hunt Johnson, Ask Janis Editorial
Book Midwife: Carrie Jareed

Printed in the United States of America

Come and sit by my side....
Do not hasten to bid me adieu.

—*The Red River Valley,* of uncertain origin, 19th century

CONTENTS

INTRODUCTION

One hundred years ago, or even fifty years ago, there would be little need for me to write this book. In those days, we grew up with death. We visited bedsides and sat vigil. Even as children, we saw our grandparents, relatives, and friends die. We watched, participated, and learned how people dealt with death and dying.

Today, medical advances have distanced us from dying. Doctors focus on defying death and keeping us on this planet longer regardless of our condition. We have turned over care and treatment of the dying to professionals. We don't like to talk about it. People die away from us, out of sight and perhaps out of mind. They often live out their remaining days away from family, in long-term care facilities or in hospitals. Sometimes they die alone. And we are afraid of this. But sooner or later, we will need to face our human mortality—in ourselves and in other people. I know, because I've been there.

I suppose the nearer events of my journey—which occurred in rapid succession—were the death of my husband; the death of my favorite aunt; and then an ad in a local paper seeking singers for a new choir whose mission would be "singing for those at the thresholds of life." Yes, I tell myself, those were pivotal moments which cumulatively steered me to find my place at the side of people who are dying.

Yet my mind wanders as I feel there is something deeper, something from a longer-ago time driving me. As I let go of struggle, what surfaces is an image of me as an 18-year-old college sophomore, volunteering at a social services department of a county general hospital.

On this day, the director gives me a list of patients whom I am to visit. I have no additional information: not who they are, not their medical condition, and no suggestions for what to say or how to approach them (this last one I take note of now, in hindsight, across five decades of elapsed time). I have only a name and a bed number.

The moment came when I visited Jim.

It is a large, open ward. Beds are arranged along each wall with no privacy between them. Additional occupied beds float in the middle of the space. I do not know how many names I was given, or how many visits I was to make. Indeed, I confess I remember visiting only this one older gentleman, alone in the middle of the room. He listed to one side, almost off his pillow.

I do remember darkness, as though too many light bulbs had burned out, and they had not been replaced. I feel my hesitancy, perhaps anxiety, too. I know the atmosphere is affecting me. Suddenly I feel unprepared to do what I had been asked.

It wasn't that I hadn't been around old people or sick people—or even dead people. I was raised at least as much by my grandparents because both my parents had to work. Being with Gram and Gramp put me in contact with lots of older folks, some who were sort-of-relatives and some who were just, well, other old folks. When I was 16, a girl my age from our youth group died. We held a service and I remember her lying in the open casket. My grandmother died the following year.

Now in the hospital it is just me with no adults to fill in the silence. So I begin, tentatively. I expect I said, "Hi. My name is Linda." I do not remember if there was any getting-to-know-you banter between us. But what I do remember clearly—even to this day—is what he said. And I recall my reaction.

If this were a movie, the sound would rise, the lights would brighten and the camera would move in for a close-up of his face as Jim uttered these words, "You know, I am dying."

Whoa. No, I did not know he was dying. I see myself standing on his left side, holding a flower. (*Was I supposed to leave a flower with each person?*) Silence. I cannot speak. I feel myself take in a quick breath. How do I respond? "I'm sorry" seems lame, but I have nothing else. More silence. Then, to say something, yes, I say, "I'm sorry."

What happened next has faded from memory. My sense is that I did not stay long at his bedside. And that I did not make any additional visits—that day or any other—to Jim or to anyone else. I was shaken. I did not know what to do. I felt helpless and unprepared. At that point, I turned away from those who were dying.

Later in life I turned again—but this time back toward death. I learned what happens to people when they die, how they feel, what they experience, and what they need to receive from others when they're dying. I also learned what I can really do to help. I know it takes courage to confront these things and work it all through in our own minds. But it's possible to find that courage through understanding, experience, and education.

In this guide, I share what I have learned and experienced so you will be better prepared than I was. I begin by offering you a broad-brush foundation of the need for help. You will learn about those who need you and why we do well to be at their side as they are dying.

I tell you what happens physically, mentally, and emotionally to us as we begin to die. I share remarkable and true stories about what can happen as death nears, and then afterward. I also make you aware of cultural, religious, and other differences among us, because they have a huge bearing on how we deal with death and dying.

Next, I tell you what you can actually, realistically, do to help someone who is dying. I offer specific actions you may take, whether the person has just been diagnosed or is closer to death. When there are conflicting viewpoints, uncertainty and no one correct answer—which I suggest is often—I offer ten guidelines to keep in mind. I describe music's healing power and bedside singing. In the final part, I show you how you can prepare yourself to serve with confidence at the bedside of a family member or a stranger. There *is* a great deal you can do.

I trust you will find this helpful when you have to confront death in your own life—with the death of people close to you. And when your own time comes.

I hope you will be comforted by the stories I share. Every story in this book is true. I either participated and witnessed them or can vouch for the individuals whom I interviewed. I have changed names, or use only first names to protect their privacy—even of those who are no longer living. (You may have your own stories to share with me. I welcome hearing from you at Linda@thecouragetocare.com.)

I also hope you will consider visiting with others whom you don't necessarily know, perhaps in a hospice or as a volunteer in a long-term residential care facility. Or with people who are living entirely on their own.

I suspect you will discover more about yourself, too, as you read through and work through this handbook. You may uncover in yourself (as I did) the particular special personal skills or talents you possess that you can uniquely use to offer others the comfort they need. Clearly, there's a need for this work. And it takes courage to confront this work. But here's the thing: It's a blessing to you to give of yourself and it is a blessing for the one dying to receive you. You become blessings to one another, as I, myself, have found joyfully to be true. I wish you well, wherever your path leads. Blessings on all our journeys.

—The Berkshires, Massachusetts, June 2020

PART ONE

THE NEED
FOR HELP

CHAPTER 1

Why People Need You to Be with Them When They're Dying—And Why You'll Need This, Too, One Day

Your pain is the breaking of the shell of your understanding.
—*Kahlil Gibran, poet, writer, artist*

As humans, we seek companionship and interaction; we need a human connection. Didn't the poet John Donne write, "No [one] is an island"? Not to mention reports and studies that show how important physical touch and hugs are for healthy development.

On any day, at any age, there are children, women, and men who wait for a visitor to bring a smile and notice them with a few moments of personal attention. There are caregivers who need a respite. There are persons who live alone at home or who find themselves for short or longer periods of time housed in residential care facilities for one ailment or another.

This last group is the one that is growing—and quickly. Ten thousand people turn age 65 each and every day. That translates to seven people reaching 65 each minute. This baby-boomer generation—of which I am a part—represents almost 80 million Americans who may be aging out of independent living and into a variety of elder-care facilities. Not only aging but also medical events—including stroke, cardiovascular problems, effects of dementia or Parkinson's, or other long-term maladies—can cause older adults to lose their ability to care for themselves.

When there is someone at our side, challenging times become more bearable. Indeed, an oft-repeated lament of the dying is how they feel alone and isolated from family and from friends. Once an integral part of a myriad of human networks, they recognize the loosening and then dissolving of connections. Persons who were at one time close may communicate less frequently until, one day, they send their last missive. By remaining close to someone who is ill or aging, however challenging that may become for us, we show we value both the person and the relationship.

People who are dying may need you to reassure them. A companion offers an ear to listen, a hand to hold and a heart to love. The dying may voice their fears, worries, regrets, disappointments. They may need to work out how—or if—a strained relationship can be repaired.

They may need you to show them that their life had meaning. Yes, they are dying but now is only a portion of their life. You can talk about the *whole* of who they are—their entire life, including its accomplishments and legacy. This is hard, necessary work to sever the umbilical cord to everything and everyone of this life.

Witnessing another's living with dying offers you an opportunity to consider how you would fare when your time comes. Each of us chooses our way of living. Each of us may choose our way of dying. There is no judgment here. As the song goes, "*I say tomayto, you say tomahto.*" We might ask now, "What would I do during my last months? What is most important to me?"

Watching someone else die pushes us to face death, to admit we are mortal beings. For Buddhists, remembering we will die is a daily practice. For more of us, death is the last thing we want to think about. "It's morbid" or "I'm too young to think about dying" are typical. But we all will die one day—for some of us, when we are very young. Thinking about death, our beliefs, and the natural continuum of life can move us to appreciate, now, each breath we take.

Exercise

Slowly look around you. Notice what is alive and will die. Be sure to include yourself. Notice the pattern of life.

When we are with the dying, we witness the wonder and awe of dying. We are privileged to experience the life force leaving a physical body, just as we are privileged to experience the life force entering a physical body at birth. We marvel at the miracle of birth when the body, itself, knows how to bring a new physical life into being. We can marvel, too, at the miracle of death when the body, itself, knows how to end our physical being.

When we sit with someone, we have a front-row seat to this mysterious and precious transition. Being present at someone's death may broaden our view of the meaning and essence of death—and of life. Although not everyone's dying is exactly the same, we discover a common trajectory of physical decline, accompanied by an energetic expansion. We may feel a shift in the atmosphere of the room. The life force—by whatever name we give it—that flows through us also flows through the one in front of us—until it doesn't. Before, we had a physical connection; now, there is a spiritual connection with the one who has passed on. This is the intimacy of death.

As spirit, we are one. Whether family, friend, neighbor, congregational member, caregiver, or stranger, our roles separate us but our human and spiritual nature binds us. As we live, and as we die, we have the opportunity to walk together toward the intimacy of death.

Who might need you? Let's meet them.
Your family
Love 'em or not, you're related, and that counts for something. The older ones likely have known you since you were born or at least for most of your life. If they did not hear *from* you, then perhaps they heard through the family grapevine *about*

you. Perhaps they received a family photo that included your smiling or grimacing visage on a card or enclosed annual letter. Whether or not you are close, they know of you and you know of them.

And then comes the news. Have you heard? Uncle Bert is getting forgetful. Aunt Betty had a stroke and cannot talk. Cousin Jack had to have a hip replacement, knee replacement, eye surgery. Dad has cancer. Perhaps because these are the people who are the closest to us, hurts are more hurtful, and happy times more joyous.

Likely you are not close to each person to the same degree, but that need not stop you from reaching out. When you do, reach out without expectation. Even with relatives—as in any relationship—it takes both persons to be open and willing to connect. It takes both to want to continue to stay in touch. Perhaps this will be the one moment of connection between you; that's OK. Coming from a sincere, heart-centered desire to share another's pain is all you need to do. This too takes courage, to make the first overture, to take the first step.

Your friends

At some point in life, friends take center stage. After all, these are the ones nearer your own age. The ones with whom you have fun. The ones who may know us better at this time in life. Although some will be better friends than others, it's a different circle of persons who for a time become like family.

Like family, there is a level of connection. You share

disappointments and dreams. You share good news and sad news. Likely you will know when something goes wrong, whether it's a relationship, an employment opportunity, or a disturbing medical report.

When a friend shares such news, how do you respond? This moment is an opportunity and a challenge. How strong is your friendship? How might you help or support your friend? For how long are you willing to be a steady presence?

Your neighbors

By neighbors we refer to the folks who live near you. (Later we consider the biblical notion of neighbor.) These are the people next door, on your block, or in your neighborhood. How interested are you in your neighbors? Do you know them? Who is in the family? Do you know the broad outlines of their lives? Who lives alone or might need assistance?

To care for our neighbors we must be willing to meet them. Some of us—including me—enjoy and seek out face-to-face encounters. Others prefer electronic forms of communication—keeping a person at a physical and perhaps also at an emotional distance. While technology has its place, particularly when in-person encounters are inadvisable, how might we encourage non-technological relationships? With illness or age, bodily movements may become restricted and mental faculties diminished, thus interfering with a person's ability to use or understand technology. How do we reach out in ways that will connect the generations?

Congregational members

In a spiritual community, we are likely to hear the oft-repeated message to "love your neighbor," "visit the sick," and "take care of others." Even here, with all good intentions, it may be challenging to create relationships, particularly in larger communities. Indeed, decades ago this understanding gave rise to a small group or small community movement within some faith traditions. The hope was for members to build closer community within their group and feel a greater sense of belonging by creating small clusters.

When we are ill and declining, how might our faith communities reach out and sustain us? When a time comes that we can no longer participate as we once had, we hope others will visit us, making sure that we, who are alone, are drawn into the wider family of which we earlier had been a joyful, full participant.

This is our hope. This is our desire. To not be forgotten, isolated, or dismissed as useless. To be remembered and loved. To contribute, and to be asked to participate as we are able. We hope to receive visitors so as to feel—and actually continue to be—part of a circle of community until our last breath.

Caregivers

Caregivers bear the brunt of caring for the dying. Every day—from grocery shopping and preparing meals to bathing, dressing, and medications—stress and worry weigh heavily on their shoulders. They wonder, "Am I doing enough? Am I doing it correctly?"

In the United States, the vast majority of care that allows elders to live in their own homes is provided by unpaid family members. With the older population increasing and living longer with chronic disabling conditions, particularly dementia, more families will face more challenging situations. In addition, delayed childbearing and longer life expectancy have given rise to what is called the "sandwich" generation, of which I am a part. I was—until both my parents died—sandwiched between the competing demands of my own children and those of my aging and chronically ill parents. Another complicating factor, which was true for me, is that women are more likely the ones who are looked to for caretaking at a time when more of us are also employed. The increased demands on our time and the constraints on our availability increase our stress and worry over meeting everyone's physical and emotional needs.

The work of caring can seem never-ending. One gentleman I visited had a bell. His wife Donna said she couldn't be out of sight or he began ringing for her. It is often the wife who is the caregiver—almost 15 million according to 2015 data—trying to meet the needs of her spouse. When dementia is the diagnosis, the challenge of care is aggravated as the disease progresses. Tammy laments how her husband continues his decline. Watching him not remember how to put on clothes, and even seeing him become highly agitated and threatening, she feels the stress and anxiety of the loss of heretofore known patterns and behaviors.

Caregiving *is* stressful and exhausting. Studies show that the health of caregivers is compromised by their selfless efforts on behalf of another. Yet we wish to do the best we can. We wish to take care of our loved ones in our home for as long as we are able. Offering respite care that enables the caregiver to rest is an increasing need.

Residents of long-term care facilities

Tucked away, residents may be far from their familiar life and faces, activities, privacy, and freedom of movement. The number of Americans aged 65 and older is projected to nearly double from 52 million in 2018 to 95 million by 2060. In addition, it is expected that by the time we reach age 85, one in two of us will suffer from some form of dementia, thereby fueling a steep rise in the need for elder care.

Who looks after our family members? Increasingly, strangers. Try as we might, family may not be available as economic and familial changes force relocation to a distant area. Even when we live nearby, personal responsibilities vie for attention and we rely more often on staff to give our loved ones the care that in earlier times was provided by extended family.

Realistically, residents do not receive as much personal attention as they might were they living in a home setting. Facilities are hampered by employee shortages, low wages, changing health care regulations, insurance reimbursements, and profit goals. I would like to believe that most health care facilities do their best—putting the most positive outlook on the situation—for their residents and for their staff. Of course, those persons who are able to afford the cost of a private facility or private home care may fare better, but that is not most of us.

One day, when your loved one's physical or mental condition suggests that supervision is prudent, she may need to be moved into a long-term residential setting. There is no 1:1 ratio of staff to resident. One former nursing home employee told me she was responsible for the care of 10–15 residents during her 12-hour shift. I have witnessed residents parked with their walkers or wheelchairs, lined up in a hall at a nurse's station. Other residents sit and watch television in their rooms. Some, still ambulatory, make their slow, repetitive journeys up and down hallways.

The facilities do what they can to schedule stimulating activities. One day someone's pet may visit. Another day there is a sing-a-long or movie. There are arts and crafts and holiday-themed events. Bingo is popular. Not all residents choose to come. Not all residents are able to come. And if they all said yes, would there be sufficient space to accommodate them?

Despite even best efforts, residents crave more personal attention than is available. Who has time to spend with just one person? Residents wait for someone who will look them in the eye, who will listen, and say, "Yes, I will come back." Someone who smiles, makes them laugh, makes them feel better just by paying attention to no one else but them. After one visit in particular I felt especially burdened by the scenes I had witnessed. I turned to poetry, trusting it would express a feeling tone which prose could not.

They sit
still
sad-faced
silent
hoping
to be chosen
to be noticed.
Hoping to win the daily lottery.

Those who are near death's door

When I tell people what I do, I frequently hear, "Oh, I could never do that!" as though dying were unnatural, scary, contagious. But you know what? You will die. I will. We all will, even though we know neither the day nor the hour. Dying is part of living, as much as we may wish to banish it from our consciousness.

When I was still new to bedside singing but confident enough to be a song leader, our group of three visited a nursing home. We were not visiting anyone in particular. We followed our then-typical practice of walking the halls, poking our heads into a room and asking whether the resident would welcome a visit and a song.

As we began walking down one dimly lit hallway, I heard loud, rhythmic, harsh sounds. They came from a gentleman who was alone in a bed positioned near the window at the far end of an otherwise empty linoleum-floored room. We went in and sang.

I felt conflicted about whether to stay or leave. The other singers were ready to leave; I wanted to stay. But that day my role was to shepherd us through this visit. I acquiesced and left Dale's room, with his throat sounds in my ears. I had learned what a so-called "death rattle" can sound like, and this was it.

I realize, now writing this, that Dale's circumstances may have made the other singers uncomfortable, just as I had been decades earlier at Jim's bedside. I had learned much and changed since Jim, however, and wanted to stay and be present for Dale. I knew Dale was moving closer to his death. I returned early the following morning but it was too late; he had taken his last breath during the night. I regretted not visiting earlier, and wondered whether he had died alone.

You could be at someone's bedside. You could prevent that person from dying alone. Dr. Atul Gawande's *Being Mortal* promotes just this—a "no one alone" movement to ensure that the dying have someone at their side during this precious time. I also envision a companion gesture of No One without Song™ whereby singers offer comforting melodies as death approaches.

Today, 80 percent of Americans say they prefer to die at home. Data shows that the reality is that 80 percent die in acute care hospitals or nursing homes, although the at-home numbers are climbing. I ask, "Who will be with them? Who will reassure them with sacred silence or soulful song?" Can you hear their silent plea as they draw ever closer to their final breath?

I wasn't chosen
now
speechless
stiffening
surely
I won't be chosen

Still

I wait

breath s l o w s

I hope
for
one
last
chance
to be chosen
to be noticed.

Are you there?

PART TWO

WHAT YOU NEED TO KNOW ABOUT DEATH AND DYING

CHAPTER 2

What Happens to People Physically When They Are Dying, and at the Point of Death

Who thinks of death, until it arrives like thunder.
—from a peche (a Tibetan manuscript of lamas' poems)

What did you imagine when you read the word *dying*? Perhaps you will see someone in a state commonly referred to as "on their deathbed." The person is lying down, with closed eyes and sallow complexion, taking periodic, shallow breaths. And yes, you may see someone similarly situated, particularly if you sit vigil.

The word *dying* can describe a wide and even healthy-looking set of circumstances. For example, someone who has just been given a terminal diagnosis is dying, but may move about the day as though he had no care in the world. From the outside, we might not see a sign that announces, "I'm dying," despite what may be churning on the inside.

For each of us, the experience of dying is individualized; it is our own. We may have the same type of disease but it progresses differently. We may have the same religious affiliation but we carry and hold that connection differently. We may have family nearby but relationships have their own melody played out over time. And yes, we each have our own perspective on life and living, on death and dying, expressed through the lens of our personality and beliefs. What follows is a general introduction to the physical process of dying.

Four ways to go

We learn there are fundamentally four paths leading toward death. One day, we'll find ourselves on one. Let's have a quick look.

Sudden death is, well, sudden—unexpected and fatal. The cause might be heart-related, brain-related, or blood-related. If our heart rhythm is abnormal or erratic, or the heart stops beating suddenly, we may die, like my grandma did. Walking on the New Jersey boardwalk, she felt tired and sat down to rest on a bench overlooking the ocean. When she rose to continue, she gently slumped onto the boards, dead. Strokes or blood clots may also cause sudden death.

A second cause of death is a terminal condition, or what is also called today a "life-limiting" condition. While medical research searches for cures, terminal illnesses evade treatment.

Our progression toward death may be rapid or drawn out, but we cannot avoid the inevitable conclusion.

When our organ systems fail, we experience another way to die. It may be our respiratory (lungs) function, renal (kidney) function, or cardiac (heart) function that goes kaput. With any one of these essential operators deteriorating, our days are numbered.

Most of us will die of frailty. This state of health is also known as "the dwindling," or simply "dying from old age." Over time, our movements slow and our abilities shrink. Our body wears out like tires that no longer support a vehicle on its journey. Yes, we are living longer than ever before, but eventually the mileage on our body becomes too great to overcome.

Early indicators

One day, you—or more likely someone else—notices something is not quite right. Your gait is off, or there's a new pain that won't go away no matter how many over-the-counter painkillers you take. Finally, you seek a medical opinion. At this stage, the hope is for a cure—or at least management of—a chronic illness.

These early decisions revolve around the physical impact of the symptoms on your ordinary daily life. Discussions focus on treatment options and their risks and potential benefits. Ask direct questions and push hard for honest, direct answers. Yes, you do want to know the bad news—sooner rather than later—if you hope to make the remaining time of your life as full and meaningful as possible. When the decision is made to focus on comfort care, including the management of pain—if any—and complementary services, then you, with your body, your family, and friends, embark on the dying journey.

The long stretch

How long does dying take? It depends. It depends on the underlying medical diagnosis and its progression. Sufferers of ALS live for several years. Persons with dementia may live for many years, albeit with a steady physical and mental decline compounded by sundowner symptoms of agitation or even violence late in the day.

It depends on when the condition is discovered. A relative was diagnosed with lung cancer and succumbed two weeks later. My widowed, great uncle who lived alone had prostate cancer with which he lived for months into years. I wonder with a smile whether his daily cocktail helped him. Others have far less time. Regardless of the medical diagnosis, some persons will outlive their prognosis; others not. It just depends.

It may depend to some extent on our readiness to die. We seem to have some allowance to confront damaged relationships, celebrate an upcoming event or complete some final, important tasks. My husband wanted to write a last essay and see his four children again. When those were accomplished, he announced he was ready to die. Three days later he took his last breath.

The dying process may be influenced by other intangibles. I say *may*—because we cannot definitively prove, for example, that bedside singing and music or other complementary modalities, personal attention, or pain management extend life beyond what it might have been had those factors been absent. Persons live longer—sometimes much longer—than expected, and others die more quickly than expected.

Signs that death is closer

We notice physical changes. Even so, death does not send us a text with a departure date and time. Someone dying may yet have weeks—even months or years—of living. Nevertheless, as we inch nearer death, our family and friends will notice a gradual shift in focus inward. We also sleep more, grow weaker, and eventually lose our appetite.

A dying person withdraws. Think about the necessity of this. When we are leaving this physical world and relationships behind, we need to separate from all of it. And so we lose interest in matters of living. Now, we turn away from television or activities, and we want fewer or no visitors—perhaps not even our pets. Too often, family and friends interpret this period of withdrawal as an indication of loss of love. That is not the case. The dying know they must leave, despite their profound love of treasured relationships. Withdrawal makes the leaving possible.

I recall a day when my husband asked to have the priest visit and offer what in today's Roman Catholic terminology is the Sacrament of the Sick. (In earlier times, this was called the Last Rites, a name which many believers continue to use.) So the priest, the deacon, our four children, their significant others, and I were all gathered around the hospital bed. The rites were given, the prayers were said, and then a hush fell over the room. You could hear the proverbial pin drop as we waited for his last breath. Startling us all, my husband laughed, opened his eyes and said, "There's too much emotion. I can't go now. There's too much emotion." Emotion holds us. It is this emotional attachment of love and care that we need to stretch to the breaking point—and then break—to be free to move on.

As our energy levels diminish, we sleep more. Indeed, we may sleep 14–18 hours each day. We also see changes in sleep patterns. Now sleep comes regardless of time of day. When awake, particularly upon first rising, we may seem confused. As some persons have reported, when they open their eyes they don't know whether they are "there or here."

Our strength deserts us and we fatigue quickly. Our voice becomes weaker, quieter. We need increasing assistance with routine tasks. Eventually we may not be able to pick up a glass for a drink or a fork for a taste of our favorite food. Personal care becomes more of a challenge. One day will not look like another.

Loss of appetite and the ability to swallow are big ones for families. Food is so intertwined with nurturance and love that we want to continue feeding someone. We want our loved ones to keep eating, believing food alone will keep them alive. I recall a moment when I looked in on my aunt and witnessed a home health aide attempting to force feed her, despite my aunt's turning her head and keeping her mouth closed. I knew what my aunt's body knew: A body that is shutting down does not require food and drink. You wouldn't gas up a wrecked car, and you don't feed a body which will soon be left behind.

Indeed, forcing someone to eat or drink may actually create harm and pain, because our elimination system is slowing and shutting down. Our body cannot rid itself of food. And when we can no longer swallow, forcing food and drink will likely cause coughing or choking.

An explanation for youngsters

What will it be like when you die?

Have you watched a pet die? He slows down, and eats less. He doesn't want to play. He may go into a corner or stay in his bed. He sleeps more and more. One day he doesn't wake up.

It's the same with people. Our body knows what to do. We don't want to play as much. We feel more tired and sleep more. We don't feel like eating. We eat and drink less and less... and then we stop. Then we sleep all the time. This is normal.

"Nearing death awareness"

Persons who are dying may begin to see things or know things. Maggie Callanan in *Final Gifts* calls this "nearing death awareness." It is not unusual for dying persons to have conversations with unseen visitors. You may witness your friend or family member staring at a place, gesturing or mouthing words, seemingly talking to an empty space in the room. These may be deceased relatives, religious figures, or angels. Others report visions of gloriously beautiful vistas, with colors vibrant beyond description. Doctors Peter Fenwick and Elizabeth Fenwick accumulated and commented upon thousands of these narratives in *The Art of Dying*. These experiences invariably leave the person feeling peaceful, happy, reassured, and comforted about what will occur at death.

There seems to be a truth with regard to unseen visitors. There seems to be a truth to the knowingness of another side. There seems to be a truth to our having some control over our leaving. There seems to be a truth to the ease with which we lift from our physical bodies. There seems to be a truth that when our days are short, we see with greater clarity that what we call life and what comes next are connected points on the same continuum:

> David tells of his last visit to his mother, Corinne. As he entered her darkened room, he left the door open behind him so the light from the hallway could stream in. After greeting her son, Corinne pointed behind him, said, "They're there," and began struggling to get out of bed and join them. David quickly reminded her that she had a broken hip, which she seemed to have forgotten. When asked whom she saw, Corinne named deceased persons she knew.

A son describes this exchange with his father, who began seeing things as he moved closer to his death:

> Dad reported seeing an army. He'd look up at the ceiling rafters. He was following something as he would a tennis match, back and forth. There was something up there and he was engaged in it.

Dad asked me, "Do you see it?" And I'd say, "See what?" I was fascinated and wanted to encourage him. "See what? The army up there! They aren't fighting; they're making plans." That was about five days or a week before he died.

As the following stories further suggest, there seems to be a truth to the shifting consciousness of "here" and "there," the closer we come to death:

While my husband Lloyd rested one afternoon in his hospital bed, I worked a crossword puzzle. Working a puzzle—in ink—was something we did together. One of us would begin and then hand it off to the other. As I was taking my turn, he raised his head off the pillow.

"Did you walk past the bed?" he asked. "I saw someone walk past the bed on the window side."

"No. I'm sitting, working on the crossword."

He lay back on his pillow.

Later he volunteered, "You know, I can feel the doors opening. I don't know where I belong anymore—here or there."

A mother whom I knew through my children reported a similar dislocation as she lay dying. "When I open my eyes, I don't know where I will be," she explained. "I look for nurses. When I see them, I know I am still here."

Is death that simple, to wake up and be "there"?

This is also a time when a dying person may begin to talk of travelling. The words may indicate travel directly, as when someone is anxious to pack a suitcase or make certain they have their tickets. Others may use suggestive language reflecting a familiar aspect of their life. An example of this kind is a gentleman who spent time on the water and announces he needs to set sail. Callanan encourages us to pay attention to the language of the dying. Their choice of words may alert us that their departure is drawing near.

Bursts of energy

It is not unusual for people to have a surprising and unexpected burst of energy as death nears. They may have been unresponsive—that is, not talking, not moving, with eyes closed. Suddenly, they are alert, or kicking, or trying to get out of bed. Some of these behaviors seem such a startling turnaround that family may believe the person has had a reversal and will be going home soon. Manny's daughter recounts his unusual exercise routine just three days before he died:

> I started reading about the last three months and how they really pull in and sleep and all those things; it was classic. The last two weeks we had home hospice. My dad was always exercising like Jack LaLaine, so it was weird to see him like this.

So he's on his deathbed and we asked a hospice physical therapist to come and see if he could do physical therapy. The guy comes, and he's saying, "Raise your right leg, raise your left leg, five times, three times, raise both your legs. Do this, do that. Do your shoulders." My dad completely comprehended and he did all the exercises. He was awake and did his entire workout!

Then there's the story of a young man who was taken to the hospital. No one guessed he would die that evening, considering the strength he exhibited that afternoon. A friend tells the story:

Douglas was in this coma and then he got out of bed and stood up and we could not stop him. There were like five or six hospital staff and nurses and nobody could stop him; it was like superhuman strength. The best all of us could do was corral him— he wasn't a big man—in the bathroom. It was just extraordinary to see that life force.

Another account comes from Mariano's daughter, who tells this story about her father who had remained, unmovable, in bed. Then he made a sudden, strong gesture—raising his clasped hands as though in prayer. That movement and that particular gesture will stay with his daughter always. She describes the day before his last:

The priest comes, and we are praying and telling my dad it's OK to go. With his ALS, he hasn't been able to move his body parts at all. Then all of a sudden he's kicking his legs up, and that's strange. So right in that moment he picks his arms up and he does this: clasps his hands together, thrusts them out, and holds them up in front of him. It didn't make sense. This part felt like, you know you hear about seeing the light [her voice cracks]; maybe he saw the light, or saw God. Whatever it was, he did this. It seemed like a miracle.

Tales of unexpected movements are common. Many accounts describe otherwise unresponsive patients who begin moving their legs as though walking. A few even summon the strength to climb—out of bed and over a bedrail—and take a few steps. All of this is normal. Are these bursts of energy in preparation for separating from the body? Following these unexpected movements, the body tends to calm down, and soon after dies.

Being with someone nearing death brings us, too, nearer death and an afterlife—if we believe in one. At bedside, we visit someone moving toward an ever-thinning veil separating worlds. Remember the scene from the film *Field of Dreams* where the character of Horace Mann is invited to go into the field with the dead ballplayers? James Earl Jones is giddy, excited—and apprehensive. He stretches out his arm toward that Iowa cornfield and then jerks his arm back. With a last laugh—and likely a deep breath for courage—he walks into the corn and slowly disappears.

The more opportunity we have to be at bedside, or to read or hear stories about another's bedside experiences, the more this weird-seeming stuff becomes familiar and natural. The similarities are remarkable. The stories sound like different versions of the same essential narrative. I wonder how our individual and cultural attitudes about death might change if we used obituaries as public witness to share not only the accomplishments of the deceased but also to recount the variety of amazing experiences we observed as they approached death.

Active dying

Finally, there is the time of active dying—the last hours to a few days of life. During this period your loved one may not move at all. You won't know whether he is asleep, in a coma-like state, or resting deeply with closed eyes. Some individuals will be absolutely still but with eyes somewhat open. Even so, the eyes will not move; they may be glassy, and seem to be staring into space. Nevertheless, it is believed that for the dying, hearing is the last sense to leave during this biological dying process.

You may notice changes in elimination and blood flow. With diminished intake, urine becomes concentrated and may emit an odor. I've heard of folks placing charcoal under the bed or using incense to mask smells. As blood flow slows, patches of skin may discolor as blood pools in an area. Also, the hands and feet may become cool to the touch.

What you may notice most of all are changes in breathing. Breathing patterns become faster or slower, in cycles. You may hear more labored breathing, sometimes called "the death rattle." Although it may be disturbing to hear, it is not painful. The sound is caused by the breath passing over saliva that accumulates in the throat because the person can no longer swallow. For some, like my aunt, the very-near-death body takes fish breaths, in which the mouth silently opens and closes…and then doesn't. Death has come.

Timing our dying

It is intriguing to speculate about whether and to what extent we have control over how or when we die. It is not unusual to hear of individuals who wait until a certain significant date. My husband, Lloyd, after saying he was ready to die, waited until a niece arrived, and then waited until the following morning, which was The Feast of the Assumption. He had been a cradle Catholic (a Catholic from birth), had spent ten years in seminary, and often said the *Memorare*. This Roman Catholic prayer asks the Blessed Virgin Mary to intercede on behalf of the penitent for help and protection. It concludes:

> Inspired by this confidence
> I fly unto thee
>
> Oh Virgin of virgins, my mother;
> to thee do I come….

Was Lloyd able to wait until he could intentionally fly to her on her feast day?

From my asking, I quickly developed a collection of similar accounts. The heartfelt rememberings include staying alive until someone's wedding or an approaching birth; and an uncle waiting to give time for his nephew, who was his namesake, to complete his studies and arrive for a final farewell. Undoubtedly, you, too, have heard stories where someone appeared to time their departure after everyone left the room, or after an important event.

The following delay is quite remarkable. An aide recounts this experience, which took place at an Ohio facility, with her "miracle lady":

> She was a little African American lady—and I say *little* because she probably weighed 80 pounds. She was tiny, petite. She was a sweetheart, a "spitfire," as my grandma might have used that term. I loved her to death. When she first got here, she had a slow decline. She stopped talking to people, was sleeping more, her heart rate began to slow, other little signs like she was getting ready to die.
>
> One day—and this gives me cold chills thinking about it—I came into her room to check on her and see if maybe she wanted me to move her a little bit. She looked at me and said, "I changed my mind. I think I want to go home now." And I'm saying, "OK, that sounds good," thinking she meant going home as in dying.

But she wasn't kidding. Her heart rate went back up. Her breathing went back up. Her oxygen levels went back up. Everything went back up. It was like she really did change her mind. And she did go home.

Watching her come out of that dying process, it was almost like an instant. It was *wow!*

Lastly, there is this account from Newfoundland, Canada. Leslie narrates her mother, Monica's, remarkable reversal:

On January 4, 2001, my mother was diagnosed with Stage 4 terminal cancer, which had metastasized in her spine and ribs. It definitely didn't look good and she was given only months to live. I had just left the corporate world to start my own business helping people to heal, internally first with their inner dialogue and then externally with the incredible healing power of Mother Earth.

I immediately flew home to be with her. One of the first things I shared was, "Mom, over the last two years I've read many books about people who have survived a terminal medical diagnosis, against all odds. There's always a small percentage of people who do. Why can't you be one of them?" She thought about it for a moment, looked me in the eyes, smiled and replied, "I will be, honey!" My father, who was a pediatric radiologist at the time, had seen the CAT scan and thought I was crazy.

Over the next few months, I incorporated into my mom's daily regimen everything that had helped me heal, including slide shows of my nature photos set to calming music. Just six months after her initial diagnosis, my mother had another scan. My dad came home wide-eyed. "I wouldn't have believed it if I hadn't seen it with my own eyes. Your mother's cancer is virtually gone," he said in disbelief. It was—and she lived another 17 years!

Letting go

Finally, the dying need to let go—and so do we, the living. We must allow our loved one to leave. Complicated by distance and unfinished business, by panic over how we will survive and manage alone—and yes, also by love—it may not be easy for family to let go. Sometimes, we beg the dying to come back. And wonder of wonders, sometimes the departing soul delays and reverses course—at least for a time. A daughter shares her story:

We were all in the Illinois area and Dad was rushed to the emergency room because he was nonresponsive. His nephew and my mom started calling his name. They're calling out to him, "Come back. We love you."

Dad was taken to a room and my mom and I spent the night. All of a sudden he pops up and comes to. That afternoon he goes unresponsive again. Doctors tell us this is probably it. Our immediate family is there and I'm rubbing Dad's arm. I was thinking of my friend, who told me I have to tell him it's OK for him to go. And I couldn't do it. I couldn't say it.

Instead, I said, "We'd love to have you stay if you're interested. If you need to go we understand that, too." So I kept rubbing his arm, saying that, and the next thing you know, in Sicilian he says something that colloquially means, "come on, leave me alone." And he lifts up his arm and shoos my hand away.

I'm looking at my family and laughing because my dad could be playful and he could be stoic. I figure he's being himself. Then I stopped and really thought about the words he said, and literally, the words mean, "Leave me go. Let me go."

So I looked at my brother and sister, pulled them aside and told them that he came back last night because some family members had called him back. I say, "I think we have to tell him it's OK to go." And so we did. [She is tearing up.] Now that I'm sharing this, it's as though his passing happened twice, in a way.

Dying is a process that has commonalities—and yet it is distinct for each of us. As you understand the general physical progression, you are prepared for the coming changes. When you have questions and need reassurance, feel free to turn to your medical providers, hospice team, or an end-of-life doula who is working with you.

CHAPTER 3

How People Respond Emotionally to the News That They Are Dying

*The value of life is revealed when it confronts
death from close quarters.*
—*Apoorve Dubey, author of* The Flight of Ambition

Decades ago—in 1977 to be precise—I happened upon Dr. Elisabeth Kübler-Ross' *On Death and Dying: what the dying have to teach doctors, nurses, clergy and their own families.* (How the book came to me, I do not know. Spirit knows; another link in the chain to where I am today.) Kübler-Ross was one of the pioneers in what would become the hospice movement. She was a Swiss psychiatrist who spoke directly to dying patients, listened to their experiences, and used that knowledge to suggest better ways to support us as death nears.

These conversations led to Kübler-Ross' formulations of what are often called the five stages of grief. Within this framework, she describes common grief responses to first hearing about and then living with a terminal condition. She called these responses "coping mechanisms to deal with extremely difficult situations." Not only the one dying but also family and other close-in persons adopt these ways to cope as they journey through an illness into the dying process.

Like dying, grief is a process. When we talk of stages, it sounds as though there is some orderly progression from denial through to acceptance. There isn't. Not everyone goes through all the reactions, nor in a particular order. Like dying, grief is unique to each of us and rarely follows a predictable pattern. Indeed, we may hover longer using one coping strategy, skip over others entirely, then circle around and try a new one, or revisit one we'd previously completed. Each of us feels grief differently from anyone else.

As a visitor—whether family member or not—you enter a space where grief may hold center stage. You may be uncomfortable around people in the throes of expressing their emotions. But whether you think in terms of stages or cycles, phases or a continuum, it will be immensely helpful to understand this dimension of dying. With this in mind, let's take a brief trip through these coping strategies: from denial and anger, to bargaining and depression, and then acceptance.

Denial

I don't believe it. Never gonna happen.
When I was growing up, my dad used to say the only things certain were death and taxes. If death is certain, and we acknowledge or joke about it in this offhand way, then why do we have such a hard time talking about it? Death may be the last taboo. Instead, we pretend it doesn't exist, isn't there, nothing to bring our awareness to—until, well, until we are dead. *Then* it will be OK to talk about death.

This goes for family members as well. We may turn away, placing our hopes on a miracle, or on the next cure, or on being the one in a hundred who survives. (And sometimes we *do* survive, as you read in the previous chapter.) Our denial or the ignoring of death separates the still-living from the still-living-but-dying. Denial can make the journey more challenging for us or for a loved one.

Often, our initial response to a difficult diagnosis is shock and disbelief. On some level, we may understand. But we are not ready to hear it. We are not ready to believe it, we can't take it in, and we're certainly not ready to accept it.

Denial permits us to cope with the outcome awaiting us. It gives us time to adjust gradually to the news. How long might we deny the news? Some persons deny the outcome almost until their last breath. These individuals just can't or won't accept what is happening to them.

How might you react when confronted with someone's denial of their condition? Unanimously, we are told to avoid correcting them. Remember, denial is a way to cope, to hold one's fragile self together in a tough time. It is for you to offer support—not to burst their bubble, or to set them straight, or to make them face reality.

Each of us knows how much we can handle at any given time. Let us proceed at our own pace, however turtle-like it may seem. It is a huge adjustment to get from "I'm really healthy" to "I'm really not." As you visit with the one dying, listen attentively to catch the moment—if and when it comes—speech gives an indication of no longer denying, that they have opened the door to at least the possibility of an unwelcome outcome, and they have moved on to another aspect of grief.

Anger

This sucks! I don't deserve this!

Anger—which may be blisteringly vocal—commonly occurs as denial fades. Some folks do rage and rail against the world and anyone who stands before them. Others will seethe internally as they give everyone the silent treatment. Depending upon one's religious beliefs, this can be a time of spiritual crisis, as anger targets God or whatever Force or Entity is held in high regard. We rage, feeling betrayed that we believers are not protected and safe.

How might you react if you arrive on a bad day and you are hit by the whirlwind? Keep in mind that this behavior is normal and necessary as part of a clearing and healing process. The anger may be directed *at* you but it's definitely not *about* you; don't take it personally.

You might try this visualization I learned many years ago. It is a simple way to protect yourself whenever you are the target of unwanted and unhelpful energy.

Exercise

See yourself as a piece of glass. Be a piece of glass. Then, just as sunlight shines through glass without altering the glass itself, see the unwelcome energy flowing through you, as you remain untouched.

When you are ready—and the person seems ready—you might calmly say something. He has just expressed some powerful emotions; he may welcome your acknowledgment of his feelings. "I hear how angry you are" is an appropriate response. Avoid giving advice. Avoid filling the vacuum with false hopes or platitudes. Listen. Really listen. Sit in silence. If it feels right—depending upon your relationship—and you can honestly offer your presence, you might let him know that you will be there for him. Another's anger can push us away. Your words, your calm silence, or your gentle action—like an appropriate hug or a touch on the arm—are reassurances that you won't be pushed away; you will stand fast at his side.

Bargaining

I promise I will [fill in the blank]. *Let me live, and I'll prove it.* Many of us bargain with our preferred Higher Power at one time or another throughout our lives. We ask for better relationships, test scores, or finances—in exchange for some new behavior on our part. Of course, grief bargaining is different, since it is one of life and death, literally. This type of bargaining contains the hope that the person can successfully delay death by changing beliefs or behaviors.

What's your place in the negotiation when you hear someone bargaining? You are an observer and a listener. Clearly, you have no power to grant their wishes. If you feel you must reply, try something non-committal like, "I hear you" or "I see you would be relieved if that could happen." More often, replies aren't needed. Your quiet, compassionate support is.

Depression

Silence. There is only…silence.

At some point, a sadness or melancholy may overtake the one dying. Now, the reality of the diagnosis is hitting home, for until we believe our life is close to ending, we have no need for the sadness of this final loss. The grieving person may not want to be around others or may not feel like talking. Earlier outward displays of anger, denial, and bargaining are now replaced with inward musings of approaching death—and the loss of all the small, beautiful moments of life.

There is no need to break the silence. Repress your need to fix anything. If you are uncomfortable, recognize it as your own issue, and address it later, alone. This person has enough to deal with. Instead, pay close attention. Honor and respect the dying person's mood and inner work. They are working hard to get through this and they need space—as well as support.

You may ask, gently, whether it is a good time for a brief visit or not—and then respond accordingly.

Acceptance

It is what it is. [Sigh.]

Acceptance does not mean that we are OK with what has happened. It does mean that we accept this new state—that this illness will take us and that we will die sooner than we would like. The diagnosis and the realization are something we begin to live with.

We now live with the certainty of our approaching death. I'm reminded of a tree and a power line up the road from my house. Over the years, the tree grew out, grew around and enfolded a portion of the power line. The tree continues to live—with the power line inside it. In acceptance, we too continue to live and may live even more fully than we might have before. Yet we do so with ourselves wrapped around this dying that is now in the midst of us.

We consider too what this will mean for family and for the wider circle of which we are a part. As we settle in to this new dynamic, we adjust our expectations and our emotions, which may begin to stabilize. Not every day is great; good days still alternate with bad ones, but the good outnumber the bad.

Now, the one dying begins again to engage with others. You may be included in proportion to the closeness of your earlier relationship. He may want to spend time with his loved ones, reminiscing, telling stories, singing old songs, and looking at photographs. He may want to sit in silence, quietly following frolicking squirrels at play, watching the day turn to night, or feeling the gentle breezes sweep over his hair and skin. More profoundly than ever before, he may appreciate the simplicity and the sacredness of life.

This also may be a time to complete unfinished business, repair a broken relationship, or give away personal possessions. Others may begin a legacy project or a life review. Conversations may include an end-of-life plan detailing the type of care and environment in which to die, or planning the funeral or memorial service. As the days go by, mobility and energy diminish. Family, close friends or an end-of-life doula may help in completing these tasks and in offering support during this dying journey.

Treading lightly in the presence of dying

Grief occurs not only after someone has died but also before. As we approach death, we experience what is called anticipatory grief, that is, the suffering, anguish, and angst over the losses that are coming. Everyone within the circle of caring experiences this grief. And it isn't only the dying part. We grieve for our loss of mobility, of our independence, of our never-to-be-realized dreams. We grieve for the birthdays and anniversaries, the graduations and holiday get-togethers we will not attend. We grieve for the change of seasons, the ordinary daily routines with family and friends and the intimacy with a special someone. Perhaps, too, we grieve that only now have we fully, deeply appreciated just how precious each moment of life is.

How do we support each other in the midst of fluctuating and profound feelings? As a visitor or companion to someone who is dying—and to their family—how do we help? Showing up and being there are cited by numerous authorities and authors as perhaps the number-one caring response. Not forgetting them is a close second. (Chapters 6 through 9 offer specific suggestions.) Your calm, compassionate presence speaks volumes. You can't fix grief; you can't make it better. Bite your tongue and don't even try. You *can* turn toward grief; sitting with another who is working through the hard business of coming to terms with dying.

Our showing up helps aging and dying individuals who often feel abandoned and ignored when they are at their most vulnerable. Kübler-Ross describes the response of a hospitalized nun who was hurt when her religious sisters did not visit even though she asked them to. "It isn't right [to] beg somebody for something that I need." Will we make someone beg?

Sitting in silence and sharing each moment of the journey is a precious gift. We sing, "*We may not need words / we may not need song / we may only need / our two hearts beating.*" We may not speak in words, but with a gentle touch we speak volumes. These precious moments of silence may be the most meaningful when we are comfortable being fully present with someone who is dying.

Feeling your own anticipatory grief

While this overview is valuable, it fails to bring you to a visceral experience of loss. As part of the still-alive group, you are separate and apart from the anticipating-death group. These exercises will begin to move you from your head closer to your heart. Please take the time to work through them. You may not wish to do all of them now. But completing even one brings you closer to the day when, like those you may visit at bedside, you, too, will lose all that means so much to you.

We feel anticipatory grief when we lose something we love, something which holds value and meaning for us. Yes, that may be losing a person, but we experience loss in other ways throughout our lives. We may lose the opportunity to travel because we became ill. We may lose a job we really wanted. We may lose the ability to pursue a talent we have. We may break an item of little intrinsic value but which to us is a precious heirloom. The heartfelt value we place on something fuels our grief when it is gone and no longer part of our life.

Losing what you most cherish

What do you value that you would grieve if it were lost? There is no judgment here. Just as each of us has our favorite type of music, each of us holds our personal, cherished favorites near to our hearts. This value-based exercise is often used at hospice training events.

Exercise

Take several deep breaths. Settle into the quiet. What do you value most in your life at this time? Make your list as answers come.

Don't judge the answers; write down whatever comes up for you. Don't worry if you have not considered this before.

Review your list and consider further. What do you value so much at this point in your life that you would regret—even despair—to lose it? Choose only five. Write each answer on its own separate piece of paper. You now have five pieces of paper.

Turn them face down. Mix them up. Pick up any one and read it. Say it aloud. Why do you value this so highly? What feelings and thoughts surface? Has it stirred specific memories? When you feel complete, tear up the paper into little bits and throw them away. Repeat for each of the remaining four, until only fragments remain.

Were you able to rip up your heart's coveted desires? Obviously, your tearing up each one is a symbolic losing—perhaps forever—of that which you so treasure. Does your ability to tear and toss change as you reach the final three, then two, then one? Are you able to shred any of them? Some of us—like me—cannot bring ourselves to rip even one. I found myself physically responding, shaking my head. My mind, my body, my heart refused to comply with the directive to destroy. If I were faced with giving these up because I was dying, I would not be ready to say goodbye. How about you?

Writing final letters to loved ones

The Stanford University School of Medicine created the life review letter project. They designed templates to help us tell loved ones how much they mean to us. We can express our love and our pride. We may ask for or grant forgiveness, say thank you and goodbye. For the recipients, these are words anyone would long to hear. For us, the writers, we may replace guilt and regret with a measure of peace and completion, having reflected more deeply about our meaningful life experiences and relationships. Whether we write, audiotape or videotape our heartfelt messages, this is a worthwhile undertaking for all of us—living or dying—while we still have time.

Exercise

The first letter suggests we acknowledge key people in our life and express our pride in their achievements. Why not choose one person, hold that person in your heart and mind and then let the words flow, without editing?

The template begins:

Dear _____,

If you are reading this, it means that I have passed on suddenly and unexpectedly. Let me start by saying that I am very grateful to you for your loving care and concern.

Continue in your own words to write a letter to this important person in your life. As you put pen to paper—my preference rather than the computer, because our identifiable handwriting is a lasting piece of us—you may be surprised by your reactions. Do you permit yourself to take in that you are writing these letters in anticipation of your future death? That the people whom you address will be lost to you—perhaps even before you take your last breath? And that they may cherish these letters as keepsakes of your love and connection?

Writing your obituary (or eulogy)

What will people say or think about you as they file past your coffin or gather at a memorial service? How do you feel about who you are and your life at this point in your journey?

Exercise

Grab several sheets of paper, a pen or pencil, and set a timer for 15 minutes. Using the flow writing technique, put to paper whatever comes to mind, as a stream of consciousness. Do not edit or analyze; keep writing for the entire period of time. Write in the third person, past tense, e.g., "She was…."

This is not a final document. Consider these questions. Go with the flow once you begin.

- *What character traits describe you?*

- *How did you make the world a better place? What did you stand for?*

- *Who were significant persons? How did you impact/ change them, or how did they impact/change you?*

- *What were significant turning points, accomplishments, or regrets in your life?*

- *What inspired you—from dreams, to books, to ideas, to spirituality?*

Writing your obituary now offers a valuable review of your life to this point. If new directions seem warranted, today can be a momentous turning point while you still have time to do something. This draft version also may serve as the foundation for what is published upon your death.

Labyrinth walking

Decades ago, I was introduced to labyrinths. I continue to find peace and resolution walking their contemplative construction. We walk into our heart and spirit center as we walk into the labyrinth's center. This beneficial practice is appropriate at any time in life.

Exercise

Locate a labyrinth (or use a finger labyrinth) and focus on a significant loss you experienced, whether of a person or otherwise. Afterward, note thoughts, feelings and behaviors from that time. What helped you cope? What was unhelpful?

May these exercises enable you to become more compassionate and sensitive to the emotional upheaval a terminal diagnosis creates. Family members struggle in their own way. Each will cycle through the various coping mechanisms at their own pace. Some may never arrive at acceptance. Some may spend much of the time in denial or anger. It is not for us to judge, criticize, or correct. It is for us to be present, to allow them to express as they need to, and to accept them as they are, in their sorrow and in their grief.

CHAPTER 4

How and Why We Die Differently

Earth Mother, you who are called by a thousand names.
May all remember we are cells in your body and dance together.
—*Starhawk, American writer*

You also need to know that we die differently. Some of these differences are of our own making. Others are imposed upon us. In the worst cases, the dying encounter people who make their remaining days harrowing ones. Offensive attitudes and harsh words about who they are replace sought-after comfort with anxiety. Here, differences are barriers to dignified treatment.

In the best scenarios, the particular desires of the dying are heard and heeded by compassionate people who completely accept them for who they are. Their last days are peaceful, even joyful. They feel loving warmth as they are wrapped in a cocoon of their chosen design. Here, differences are honored and celebrated.

Cultural considerations

In unsettling times—like when we've received a terminal diagnosis—we retreat to familiar patterns. We seek solace in predictability. We take comfort in that which is known, in that which has brought us peace or joy. Always, and especially at this time, practices which wrap the dying in the warmth of reassurance, acceptance, and familiarity are needed.

One set of familiar practices may come from our cultural identity. It may come from where we are born, the language we speak, or the traditions handed down to us through generations. Others may have adopted certain practices as an adult, having read about or witnessed a custom that is appealing. Food, dress, music, and more—we take comfort in common patterns which strike some deep chord in us. Indeed, we may not fully comprehend their importance until they are absent or unavailable.

Language is one example where differences can create barriers to appropriate medical care—and concern for that person and family. Having a life-threatening illness is scary in itself. Anxiety is heightened when we are unable to understand significant medical conversations or the interplay of particular cultural beliefs. Suspicions may arise as to what is being decided, by whom, and whether it is in our best interests. How do we grasp the nuance of language? Do we know American Sign Language? Words are not always needed to convey compassion and support. But when words are needed, how do we speak so the listener can hear and understand?

Food. We eat to live; we live to eat. Whether it is family tradition to bring spaghetti and garlic bread to the hospital, or enjoying Mexico's *pan de muerto*—bread shaped to look like bones—food takes a central place in our celebrations and memorials. Foods and their preparation are woven together with heartfelt memories. Comfort food may be especially welcome at times like these. But whose food? Your tastes are not necessarily mine.

With music, your screech is my serenade. Each of us has our preferences; we resonate to those melodies we grew up with in our families, in our locales, from our generation. When we hear what we do not like and do not want, we may become agitated if we are unable to escape those vibrations. Each of us prefers hearing the sound of languages that are comforting to our ear and to our spirit.

Religious differences

Religion divides us. Believers can get pretty testy when they perceive that their beliefs are being questioned or dishonored. We all hold beliefs—examined and conscious, or unidentified and hidden. They help us navigate our place in the world, our actions toward each other, and explain a broader meaning and purpose in life.

Consider, for example, the diversity of religious language alone. We speak of God, Lord, Jesus Christ, Allah, Adonai. Then there is Mother Earth, Father Sky, Great Spirit. The I

AM, Source, Divine Providence, Cosmic Consciousness, Infinite Intelligence, The Universe, The Self, and more—or none of the above! Our choice of name corresponds to a particular worldview and to a set of traditions and observances. Whether different from or similar to our own personal beliefs, at bedside we honor the family's beliefs and language.

Religious and cultural differences influence how we grieve. For some, the family feels the need to be present, squeezing around the bed of their loved one and spilling out into the hallway even in an intensive care unit. At the moment of death, everyone shrieks and wails, as is their custom; no quiet in that hospital. The public New Orleans funeral processions have their own manner of announcing a death—from sad dirges on the way to the cemetery to upbeat numbers for dancing once the body is buried. Whatever the tradition, we remain open-minded and open-hearted to ease someone's dying and transition, according to their desires and customs.

Even when we are familiar with the tenets of a particular religion, we cannot be certain we know how someone else actually practices. For example, we may assume that because someone is currently unaffiliated with any religion, that clergy or prayer will be rejected. But people can change their mind, like a man I knew named Charlie, who requested clergy for reassurance, deciding to embrace the familiarity of traditions he'd abandoned long ago. In contrast, another family, all of whom held to their atheism, were horrified when a staff person directed a hospital chaplain to the room, assuming the family would wish prayer at their father's death.

When we ask, then we know—avoiding missteps and additional anguish for the dying and their families. Even with our family and friends, we ask rather than assume. Why? Because we change. Something we may have dismissed earlier now becomes significant. Something we have experienced may have altered our outlook. The only one who knows what is desired is the person himself. Ask, and for each individual you will discover particular preferences in that moment. Dying is a personal experience. Each of us is entitled to live our way while dying.

Judgment and bias—a deeper divide

When health care capacity is stressed and medical equipment is limited—as in today's pandemic—there is heightened concern about the rationing of care, especially to certain populations. The bias and violence against people of color and the LGBTQ community has long been public knowledge, even if not acknowledged. Individuals who are disabled are judged to have a diminished quality of life, deemed not worth saving. The old are dismissed as being burdens, with nothing left to contribute. All of them rightly worry that they will not receive the same level of medical care and concern as the rest of the population.

Personal and institutional disparities stemming from race and ethnicity are legion. Some patients distrust the health care system and its medical professionals. Can I trust what a doctor tells me? Will the doctor tell me what other treatments are available? Is the care I am receiving on par with that received by white folks, abled folks, straight folks, rich folks?

Some physicians, for example, do treat people of color differently. And there are some physicians who will include a staff member who is of the same race or ethnicity as the patient, to act as a comforting bridge. This overture tends to help a patient relax; difficult, intimate discussions about life and death tend to proceed more easily. When we visit someone's bedside, are we aware of our own attitudes and behaviors?

One way to judge a medical facility's acceptance of diversity is to look at the language of its non-discrimination statement. For example, after reading the language and noticing that a local Virginia medical facility did not include the LGBTQ community as a protected class, Patty decided to care for Paula at home. They were suspicious of the quality of care Paula would receive and of how they would be treated by staff. Offensive treatment may include staff expressing hate-filled opinions to the person seeking medical care. A facility may also refuse to acknowledge a patient's partner, withholding medical information and denying participation in life-and-death conversations. Such behaviors compound the anxiety and burden of the terminal diagnosis, not only for the one dying but also for loved ones.

Persons with disabilities also struggle with the acceptance and availability of adequate health care. Responding to a query about her quality of life, one woman who was born with limited use of her muscles and joints wrote that she is "incredibly proud" of who she is and the life she has made using a power wheelchair. She is clear and adamant about not wanting at her bedside anyone who devalues who she is. Her words are a cautionary tale whenever we encounter someone whom we label as disabled.

People with disabilities are, first and foremost, people. The Everybody Counts! program for elementary school children was designed with this people-first focus. It aims to foster understanding and enlarge the circle of inclusion. I was both a trainer of teachers and a teacher when the program was offered in my children's Indiana school system.

The fallout when race and disability collide may be deadly. Blogger s.e. smith, advocate for the disabled, writes: "What kills us…[is] the way in which society treats us. We die because we can't access basic health care, because racial disparities are amplified by disability." Indeed, today as I write this, there is a report from Texas about a 46-year-old family man—a Black man who was also paraplegic—who was hospitalized with covid-19. His treatment was ended and he died. There are allegations that the decision to withdraw medical support was based on his having a presumed low quality of life. An investigation is under way. Months before this Texas incident, the director of the federal Office of Civil Rights feared something like this could become widespread. Therefore, the director issued guidelines which he hoped would prevent states from putting the elderly and persons with disabilities "at the back of the line" for care. At the time of this writing, his office has already negotiated settlements with three states that had, indeed, planned on limiting care.

We each define our own quality of life. It is for no one else, including those of us who may one day be in a position to support them at bedside, to judge. A daughter who was her dad's health care proxy asked about his desires regarding treatment options being considered. Her dad said as long as he could eat ice cream and watch football on TV, he didn't care what shape he was in. This may seem like an extreme choice, but it was for him—not for his daughter and not for us—to make.

Who we each are as individuals

It is often said that we die the way we live. Stoic people remain stoic. Angry people, angry. Gentle people, gentle. Whether or not this is true in all cases, it bears remembering when personalities clash and tensions erupt. And when personality differences are combined with the influence of grief, the result may be a particularly difficult moment—this time. Holding our center and not taking someone else's behavior personally, we may see beyond the tumult, and understand.

When ill or dying, we wish to be known for who we are—apart from our diagnosis. We revel in the attention and affirmation of others who want to know our story and learn of us more deeply. What interests, skills, and experiences make me unique? What accomplishments make me proud? Together, we may discover and celebrate life as well as identify specific ways to support our dying.

Surely now, in our dying, our preferences can be honored. Others may be uncomfortable or disagree vehemently with our choices. But it is not their death. It is for the one dying to freely voice their vision of their last earthly days. They get to choose who will be present at their side, what music to play, what prayers or rituals will be said, and any number of other significant or silly—to our mind—details. For us, the living, we join them in our common humanity and in our oneness of spirit. We honor their wishes, whoever they are.

CHAPTER 5

What Happens at Death—and After

*[D]eath is only a horizon; and a horizon is nothing
save the limit of our sight.*
—Rossiter Raymond Worthington, *novelist,*
legal scholar, mining engineer

What happens at the moment of death—and after?
Aspects of the answer to this question are clear; others
not so much. We witness what occurs physically before us at
bedside. We notice changes in the way someone looks. We also
may feel a change in the atmosphere of the space. But the after
part, well, those answers mostly depend upon our perspective.
Yet even here there are intriguing visible occurrences that may
give us pause.

At death

Some of us—including me—speak of someone "transitioning" at what is called death. We intentionally use this language to express our belief that death is a birth into another existence— into some continuing spiritual or energetic form. Stephanie, a former hospice worker in Ohio, attempts to articulate her understanding:

> There is no question in my mind after being with so many people as they passed that there is definitely something after we pass. I can't say what it is. At the very least we are energy inside a container. Energy cannot be destroyed, it can only be changed—if you're going to get scientific about it—so there you go. When someone passes away you feel the energy shift, big time. It's hard to explain but the body, you can tell, is just a shell at that point. It's different. I wish I could find all the words in my head to describe it. It's not like a TV you turn off. No, it's completely different. When somebody passes away you can see the energy shift. That was confirmation for me, that energy inside of us—soul, spirit, whatever you want to call it—definitely goes elsewhere.

Perhaps for you this is a new perspective. Our beliefs and expectations influence our experience. It may be that you've somehow felt different or felt a difference in the room if you've witnessed someone's death—but didn't know how to explain it or name it. Perhaps at the next deathbed, you'll pay closer attention to what is happening in front of you. You never know what the next experience will be like.

Everything is energy

We learn that each of us—all of life—is energy. Remember grade-school science class and the lesson on atoms? You know—protons, neutrons, and electrons. The electrons spin around the nucleus. As a child I wondered, if I am made of innumerable atoms, each of which has space to permit the high-speed movement of electrons, how could I look solid, and why didn't I feel the energy of the movement? (I long ago learned how to feel the energy. My thanks to my first meditation teacher, Windy.)

Exercise

If you have little or no experience with energy, here's one way to feel the energy which flows through you. Be still and move your attention to your arms. Do your arms feel quiet and still? Now, standing or sitting with enough space around you, give one arm a good shake while you count to ten. Again bring your attention to that arm. Likely, you will notice the arm feels different. It may feel tingly or seem to pulsate. Your arm may feel, well, not still; something is moving. What you are feeling is the energy that flows through your body continuously—while you are alive.

Writing this section reminded me of my first encounter with energy as a college freshman. On this day, several of us were gathered in a small lounge. I have no recollection of how the session was arranged, only that I was a part of it—and I recall vividly what occurred. A senior, who was more than six feet tall and of solid build, lay on the linoleum floor. There were two of us on one side of her and two on the other. We were instructed to place just two fingers underneath her.

The senior was told to think of herself as a feather. She was as light as a feather and it would be easy to fly or to be blown about. We lifters were told the same—that we were lifting a feather, and how easily and effortlessly that would be accomplished. After a bit, we were told to lift and raise the feather. The body began to ascend. When it was more than a foot off the floor, it suddenly crashed. After collecting herself, the student explained that she realized she was moving higher. At that moment, she was no longer a feather but a thinking student; her rational mind had kicked in. What else don't we know about life—and about death?

Orbs and light

A number of years ago I attended a few sessions led by a physicist turned shaman. One of the participants brought a photo album of pictures, most taken of a Victorian home in New Jersey. The photos were covered with bright white circles. Orbs that appear to be white or silver are considered to be spirits. (Light, too, is energy.)

At the time of death we may encounter other white substances. Not limited to spheres, we may see wisps or clouds of white emanating from a body. Rita described one such experience at her brother's bedside. She writes:

> Death is a natural happening; we will all die, some of us sooner than later. I have watched my oldest brother die at 42 and my mother at 84. I am sure it was most comforting to them both that they had most of their family with them. At the time of death, it was strange to see a wisp of a cloud exit my brother's mouth as he gave his last breath.

I have also read of a stream of white flowing from the top of the head at death. Another report comes from a woman who, after her loved one took his last breath, placed her hand above his head. She said she felt a movement or flow of something, which she interpreted as energy leaving.

I unexpectedly was reintroduced to orbs while conducting interviews for this book. Kevin was narrating the story of his father's last days. When Kevin finished, I asked if he had felt his deceased dad around him during our Zoom chat. I told Kevin that I had been seeing wisps of bright white and a white ball floating in the air. Kevin replied:

> Yes, my father is often here. I can feel his energy here. It is amazing to have that perspective. I wish everyone could have that perspective. When people

come to see me, they admit they sense and feel their [deceased] parents around but put them out of their minds because it doesn't make sense in their rational world. But I know [their deceased parents] are very much around and are very aware of what's going on. We toast my dad often. He is a continuing factor in our lives.

The second instance occurred in my writing space at the conclusion of an interview with Hannah, who grew up in the Midwest and attended Stanford. She described herself as a "really grounded person, not a far-out hippie or woo-woo person at all." Moving on to stories of being with the dying, she emphasized that each experience was unexpected. "I had no clue and couldn't have made them up. No embellishments; they are just true."

As we ended our online conversation, I looked up. Silver and white orbs circled over my head. I blinked and looked again. Still there. It came to me that these were the people in Hannah's stories. I was moved to name each person. I did so, and as I arrived at the last name, everything disappeared. I know on a deep level that those folks were checking in, happy to be remembered in this special way through the stories of their dying.

Are we able—or are some of us able—to manifest after death as orbs of light, under certain unknown-to-us-now conditions? What a thought! What a wonder!

Sometimes the white-colored energies take a more distinct shape. The late Sylvia Browne was a well-known author and psychic who used her gift for healing. At large presentations, audiences began noticing a white cloudy figure standing next to her. When Sylvia realized what was attracting their attention, she introduced Josephine, her spirit guide.

Then there was Ellen, a woman I met at a writer's conference. After I mentioned this book, Ellen shared an experience she'd had with her deceased mother. Ellen explained that according to her Greek Orthodox beliefs, a person does not end earthly existence at death but waits until the ninth day when the soul meets the Creator. Traditionally, the family gathers to pray on that day so it may go well with their loved one. As Ellen prayed on that ninth day after her mother's death, she told me that her mother appeared in her room and looked just as real as I did sitting across our lunch table. Other books recount similar stories of appearances.

Rainbows

From the book of Genesis to Judy Garland singing *Somewhere over the Rainbow* to Buddhist masters' rainbow bodies, the rainbow has been and still is an exciting welcome in the sky, as well as a glorious symbol of hope and promise. Genesis 9:12–13 reassures us:

> And God said, This is the token of the covenant which I make between me and you and every living creature that is with you, for perpetual generations: I do set my bow in the cloud, and it shall be for a token of a covenant between me and the earth.

A rainbow is a symbolic bridge between all that exists. It connects Heaven—or the heavens—and Earth. It connects the spiritual and the physical, the invisible and the visible. After someone has died, it is not unusual to see a rainbow. Is this appearance a reassurance that all is well in our continuing and promised connection?

This rainbow story comes from California. The storyteller came to know Brad at San Francisco General Hospital when providing therapeutic massage to ease his pain. When Brad died, she attended his funeral:

> There was a nice service, and then a nice graveside service for the burial. And you know how they have the open pit for the casket? It was a partly cloudy day and the whole thing was over, and I'm walking away to my car with just the feelings of everything.
>
> I'm maybe 30 yards away and I feel like looking back. So I turn around and what I saw—I swear to God everything I'm telling you is literal because I don't make stuff up. This happened. There is a rainbow just stretching exactly from here to here across the grave, over the casket. There was a perfect rainbow!
>
> I just looked back, you know, like to say a last goodbye. Am I expecting to see that? Who could ever dream to see a little rainbow exactly in that little space over the casket?

There were rainbows in the sky when my husband died. Buddhist reports of rainbow bodies add another layer of mystery—and of wonder about the possibilities of joined physical and spiritual natures. Buddhist masters spend their lives focused on living the advanced practices of Buddhist teachings. And for some of these masters, their physical body disappears completely, actually dissolving into light, as they die. The process is known as the "rainbow body" or "body of light" because the final disappearance is often accompanied by rainbows or bursts of light.

I know, you may be finding this crazy and impossible to believe. But at one time it happened so frequently Buddhists began keeping records and categorized the occurrences. One 20th-century case, "witnessed by many" was a 79-year-old man who was a carver and songwriter. When he felt death approaching, he told his family to wrap his body at his death, place it in a small room and then not move it for the next week. When he died, a rainbow surrounded the house. On the sixth day, the family noticed the body had gotten much smaller. On the eighth day, when the body was to be moved for the funeral, the family found only nails and hair inside the wrapping.

Remember how you may have used a prism to show how white light passing through it produces a spectrum of color? It is from the splitting of white light that we then see the hidden colored parts that comprise the whole. At the least, a rainbow may remind us that there is more to be seen and known than seems apparent on the surface.

Having that perspective

Are these coincidences or signs of continuing life? Thinking of or feeling someone, and then getting a call that they died. A stranger appearing from nowhere to offer aid on a lonely stretch of road. A rainbow, or a cardinal, or pennies at the moment of one's dying. Depending upon your need to offer rational explanations for simultaneous occurrences, you may ignore, dismiss, or ridicule signs of another reality. How do you explain more true-life stories like these? Sally's best friend narrates:

> It took a while to figure out that Sally had a brain tumor. Then she had a brain hemorrhage.
>
> One day I came home from teaching and had to take a walk. The way the sunset was, it was just an amazing oil painting in the sky, and I started singing a song. I can't remember it now—but you know when a song just comes to you—and I was singing it and I kept singing this one part over and over and over, and I couldn't stop singing it—to this exquisite oil painting in the sky. My watch read 7:19 p.m.
>
> The next day we were talking with Sally's boyfriend. He said she died at 7:19 p.m.—and the whole thing was just so amazing. Seven and nineteen were her [favorite] numbers, too.

This next experience took place in Florida. Rebekah recounts what happened:

I went to be with my dad on the first anniversary of my mother's death. I took a walk after midnight, and had Pandora on. I was remembering the times I walked with my mom and listened to music. This one piece called *Gabriel's Oboe* was playing when she passed.

I listen to Pandora a lot, and maybe once in six months this piece plays. Whenever it comes up I listen, go "ooooh," and stop for its 2- to 3-minute length. So this night, at 12:56 a.m., what comes on Pandora but that song! And my mother had died at 12:56 a.m.! It was unbelievable. You can't explain these things.

Do the dead communicate with us? Was Rebekah's mother communicating with her? Is each of us spirit and so continue when we leave physical form, thus permitting ongoing communication? The translated lyric of *Ipharadisi*, a traditional South African melody, notes that *Ipharadisi* is "where all the dead are living." Kevin, both personally and professionally, would answer the question, "yes, the dead can communicate with us":

Two years after my dad passed, I was at a retreat in England with other mediums, and my father came through. He told me how much that it touched him for me to be with him as he was passing and for me to talk to him—not trying to avoid the subject but to be there and to meet him there. He mentioned that I had told him his brothers were there [as he was dying]. He wanted me to know that when he did cross, he did see his brothers, and how happy he was to be reunited with them.

We may receive messages from the other side not only through reputable mediums, but also through another member of the family. This daughter describes her experience:

> On the anniversary of my mother's death, I asked her if she had any messages, and she gave me one for my dad. So I'm talking to my dad—he's in his 90s, a little Midwestern businessman. So I said, "You know Dad, I want to tell you about my walk"—I was a little shy about bringing it up—and he says, "OK." So I started, and then I told him that I had a message from Mom, and asked if he wanted to hear it. "Yeah," he says. "Well," I told him, "she said, 'Where I am it's great, it's good, it's really good. And there's no time here. You don't need to rush to come to be with me because there is no time. As long as you are happy and healthy just take your time because there is no rush.'" We had five more incredible years with him. He was just shy of 98 when he passed.

Sometimes, a loved one reaches out to us, even when we haven't believed any of this stuff. It can be challenging to incorporate an unusual but real-life personal experience. We are changed—and we don't know what that means for us:

> My older brother was not a believer at all in an afterlife or anything like that, and he was really troubled by our dad's passing. A few nights afterward, my brother was sitting alone in his living room at two in the morning—and he called me later and told me—when all of a sudden he felt this amazing touch of love. And he knew that Dad was there giving him love.
>
> It was an epiphany for him; he had never had one in his whole life. It was a connection to that amazing source of energy and love. And when it dissipated he knew that Dad had been there and touched him.
>
> He told me, "I know you believe in all of this, and I never have. I had that experience and don't know what to make of it, but I do know it was Dad."

What about feeling a deceased person's energy, not in your room but across the miles?

Rosie describes what happened to her as she was on a work call one day:

> Suddenly I had the weirdest feeling inside me like something was being sucked out inside me, and so I was compulsively eating. I felt like I was trying to fill up space, that something had come out of me. An hour later, I got a call that my Uncle Vince had died.

These are but a few of the thousands of stories that abound—perhaps you may even recall similar experiences from your own life. In addition to the narratives of our sacred texts and spiritual practitioners, we have a continuity of individuals whose work reminds us of this alternate perspective. In my lifetime alone, there's been Edgar Cayce, a devout Christian whose deep Bible study led to his becoming known as "the sleeping prophet"; Raymond Moody's *Life after Life* chronicling near-death experiences; Michael Newton's research in his books on life between lives; and numerous channeled books including *A Course in Miracles*, Paul Selig's *I am the Word*, Abraham and Seth, *Heavenletters*, and more.

Leslie's account of her own near-death experience concludes this chapter, tying together energy, wonder, and death:

I had my bicycle accident. I had my near-death experience. I was in a coma. And when I came out of the coma, I understood so much about life. I understood that my six-year-old brother who was hit by a truck, that his journey here on Earth was meant to be short. I understood that my mother's journey with cancer was about my learning to embrace who I came here to be, and to start me on that journey.

After my near-death experience, I understood that we are truly magnificent beings of light, and our bodies are just tiny grains of sand in this *energy* that is us. And that we chose to come here in human form and that our bodies are vessels for our souls. So when we die, we don't die; we are just in transition. When the person we love is transitioning, they're just going back to their natural form. Their time here on Earth is done but that doesn't mean that their time here energetically is done.

I was meant to share this so others wouldn't be afraid of living while they were here, and then they wouldn't be afraid to die when the time came for them to die.

PART THREE

HOW YOU CAN HELP

CHAPTER 6

Ten Principles to Guide You

There are a thousand ways to kneel and kiss the earth.
—Rumi, 13th-century Persian poet and Sufi mystic

You want to help, but you have fears and doubts. You don't want to do it wrong. Will you upset the person dying by showing your feelings? What if you don't know what to say or what the person needs? You have so many questions and so few answers. And you'd love specific answers for your specific situation.

But each situation is different. These principles can guide you when you are confused, if you feel helpless, or if you're in disagreement with others. They come from my learning and experience. Use them as a framework for choosing what actions to take or what to avoid. As guidelines, they permit you to tailor your actions based on your own experiences, personality, and relationship with the person dying. Let Rumi remind you that there are multiple, heartfelt behaviors to being your best.

Here are ten guidelines for every day—of living and of dying.

#1 Be aware of your energy

When you enter any space, what enters is your physical and your energy body. Remember the Beach Boys' *Good Vibrations*? Perhaps using the language of vibes resonates with you more than energy. Vibes are our vibrations of energy that are of us and with us always. We are like a stone thrown into a pond, creating ripples of vibration, affecting any environment in which we find ourselves.

We give off vibes all the time. Have you walked into a room and felt happy? Have you walked into a room and felt "off" somehow? Are there spaces that make you feel sad or anxious? You are picking up on and feeling the energy left in that space from others before you. Every time we enter a space, we bring our energy body with us. We bring our thoughts and our feelings with us. The energy of our thoughts and feelings—and of our words—remains, despite our having left the room.

All persons in a room, including the one dying, mix their energies together. They find themselves in a larger energetic field. Depending upon their emotional states (refer back to Chapter 3), they may exude anger or depression. They may also be in an energetic space of profound gratitude and love. They feel and can be influenced by others' vibrations. You will feel theirs.

They will feel your energy, too. Knowing this, it is important to pay attention to what you bring with you into a room. Be conscious of your feelings—and of your thoughts.

Still not convinced about the effect of your energy on others? Dr. Masaru Emoto ran a series of water experiments to demonstrate the effect of our emotions—our energy—on our surroundings. Why water? The human body is 90 percent water. When the researcher spoke "love" or "thank you," for example, to the water, beautiful bright crystals formed. When the water was told "you idiot" or "I hate you," the water crystals were dark, irregular, partial.

It is important to be aware of the energy we bring. Bring an even energy. To be fully present, we must be aware of our internal dialogue and our feelings. What vibe are we projecting? Have we put to the side our personal concerns and distractions? Are we focusing on the person in front of us? Do we have an attitude and energy of compassion, of gratitude, of peace?

Exercise

A personal ritual—a set of repeated actions—is a valuable preparation practice to settle your energy. Put aside distractions and focus on where you are. Ask for aid and guidance from whatever Higher Place you know. Be in gratitude for the opportunity to walk with another on this intimate journey. Offer an intention, a statement of how you intend to be and what you will offer to this person. Intend to be open, accepting, and compassionate—and then enter.

From this neutral, caring space, you feel and observe each person and their interactions. If there is a sense of serenity, then you will avoid being loud and bouncy. If you feel a sense of anxiety or anger, you may send out a calm and understanding presence.

As you continue to monitor the ebb and flow of your time together, you'll notice energetic shifts. At these moments you can respond accordingly. Perhaps you'll bring your joyful self or your musical side to the fore. You will know—you will feel—when and how to be present, altering and lifting up the energy and thus everyone's spirits. Be attuned, and go with the flow—of the energy (or vibrations).

#2 STOP: See The whOle Person

I just had an image of parsing a person and keeping the parts I like. Paper dolls or LEGOs might work that way, but life and relationships do not. For us, it's all or nothing.

What do you see when you walk through the door? Changes can occur overnight, even if you have been alerted to the person's declining physical appearance and behavior. You may experience the shock of a nasty or gruff demeanor. This is not the time to gasp, retreat, or put an "oh my" look on your face. This is the time to maintain your equanimity and poise, regardless of the sight in front of you, or—to state this more accurately—regardless of how you experience the person in front of you.

Exercise

If you are unsettled by someone's physical form, try this. Focus on their eyes. Look into their eyes. See into the heart and soul of the dear one before you. See beauty shining through the outward form.

In every instance with every person, STOP: See The whOle Person. See into their center. See who they are beyond their physical, mental, or emotional state. The person before you represents only this slice of their life; this piece does not show the whole of who they are. See into their past and into their future. See their disappointments and dreams, their anxieties and accomplishments, their losses and loves. Enlarge your vision and see the totality of their human experience, which is now coming to an end.

That's the way it is at bedside, too. When we intend to offer wholehearted support, we need to see and accept the whole person, as they are—warts and all. If we cannot do that, then it's time to reconsider our commitment to this particular person. Remember, our energy—accepting or judgmental—is felt; it is noticed.

When we accept the whole person, we stand in unconditional positive regard. In being fully present, we do notice behaviors and speech, but as an observer only. Standing in high regard for all persons, we are neutral about what we see; it is what it is. We watch what disagreements may be creating distress in the family. We notice how this person acts with that one;

which relationships are easy or challenging. We see beyond how people outwardly present themselves. You may be the one person to gladden their day and see them whole—and holy—just as they are.

#3 Ask: Is this a good time?

Whether you call to chat or wish to ask about making a visit, your opening line—after identifying yourself—might be, "Is this a good time?" You want to connect. You want to help. Maybe you want to feel good about yourself for reaching out. More important, you need to find out whether you and your caring overtures can be received at this time.

The person who is dying, and that person's family, need to manage so much. Are they in the midst of a poignant moment, a tense disagreement, or an emergency situation? Circumstances change quickly.

Perhaps add, "If this is not a good time, please say so." You are giving permission to tell you to go away and to do what is best for them.

And when you are visiting or talking on the phone, be alert and recognize whether to stay or to go. (It's that energy again.) Be attuned to the other person. Be aware of your length of visit, timing, and so forth. When your presence feels uncomfortable, inconvenient, intrusive, or unwelcome, take your leave before others suggest it. And when you realize you are not in a balanced emotional or energetic space, connect to reschedule your visit. Return when you are able to offer your better self.

#4 Befriend silence

As a college junior, I was invited to participate in a leadership group. At our first meeting, the facilitator walked in and sat down—in silence. Moments passed—continued silence. Accustomed as I was to quiet, I enjoyed the tranquility. A minute or two later, a voice yelled, "So what's going on? When is this going to start?" Like that student, some of us become quite uneasy when all is quiet.

How do you handle extended silence? It is tempting to fill uncomfortable periods of silence with talk. Resist breaking the silence; let the one you are visiting do so.

Sit in silence with each other. Perhaps your company is appreciated, but someone is too tired to talk. Too many visitors and too many worries can sap our strength. Silence allows a person to slip into a nap and rest. Maybe the one dying needs silence right now—for prayer, for space to review life's choices, or for contemplating death. Breathe into the shared silence. Honor the deep unspoken connection between you.

#5 Listen actively

Yes, listen. Listening is more than sitting silently as another speaks. Deep listening is focusing on what is said; how it is said; as well as the tone, inflection, and emotions that are released or held back.

Listening actively includes giving cues that indicate we are paying attention. A nod. An "I see." Perhaps a "please say more" or "tell me about that." Ask an open-ended question. We can offer language that validates what we are hearing. Examples of neutral responses include: "Yes, I hear you." "Yes, you are in pain." "Yes, this is so much to bear." "Yes, you are working on it." "Yes, I am with you." Our response is encouraging, supportive, and non-judgmental.

The way in which we listen also gives cues as to whether we can be trusted. Are we giving unsolicited advice? Are we avoiding talking about dying and death? Are we brushing off emotions or contradicting feelings? Are we respecting and accepting the decisions, opinions, or desires of the one dying? When our loved one trusts us, she will be more willing to share the deeper parts of herself.

For several months, we visited Ann weekly. Each visit was different; she was different physically and mentally. And so we responded differently. Some visits we sang quietly. Others we sat in silence. We always smiled. One day, silent, quiet Ann began talking. We did not understand every word but we knew she was speaking of her life. For 30 minutes, she continued without a break. At the end she distinctly said, "I thought you would listen." And I responded, "Thank you for trusting us with your story." Whatever energetically had happened between us on prior visits, it culminated in her opening up in that moment and sharing what was on her heart. It was the last time we found her coherent.

When a loved one shares challenges, fears, or frustrations, it does not mean she is helpless. It does not mean she wants a response or advice. It simply and profoundly may mean that she trusts you—or wants to trust you—to be a companion who can hold her pain and confusion and grief at what she is losing too soon. Accept the way she feels. Let her figure out what she wants to do. Each of us is strong, with the answers inside us. Listen.

If you feel you must, you might offer, "If you ever want to talk about anything, I'm willing to listen." But if you make this offer, then mean it—decide that you will be available, that you will change your schedule if necessary, that you will listen—*whenever the call comes*. Either be prepared to honor your commitment or don't make the offer.

#6 WAIT before talking

It is natural for us to want to talk when we get together, but this guideline reminds us to first WAIT: Ask, Why Am I Talking? This question is especially valuable when we are nervous or uncomfortable. It is in these situations that we tend to ramble on and run at the mouth. Talking gives us something to do and steers the conversation to safe-for-us topics. Our discomfort with death can make it hard to talk about what is going on for our loved one. WAIT encourages us to face what we may be avoiding in our conversations.

WAIT prompts us to hit the pause button. We take a breath and consider why and what we are talking about. Does our listener really want to hear comparisons of illness or treatments with someone else's? Does he want to hear us talk about ourselves? Probably not, if our loved one has not asked for this information. The focus is not on us or on our needs.

WAIT also reminds us that people want to be normal and set their illness to the side. They are still alive and want to be treated the way we typically interact.

Mary was still ambulatory, getting out of bed, taking care of her basic needs and entertaining many friends in her room. At my first visit, Mary told me, "I'm dying and I'm OK with that." This she said without any prompting from me. Just a bald statement inserted in an otherwise friendly conversation you might have when visiting your next-door neighbor or friend.

What might you talk about? Notice what is in front of you. "I see you are [sitting up today; resting comfortably in bed; whatever]." Do you see photos of family? Ask about them. Are there flowers in the room? Ask about their preferences, or talk about gardens. Birds at a feeder outside the window lead to a different exchange. I asked after a handmade quilt atop one woman's bed, and I was treated to a long and lively story. Ask about memories or family traditions associated with the time of year. And, depending upon your relationship, share the moments that filled your earlier get-togethers.

WAIT and wonder who this person is. She wasn't always sick or dying. She had a life, a past, a story. Ask about and be genuinely interested in what she has to say. In turn, she may ask about you and your life. Phyllis often asked me, "What mischief have you been up to?" She wanted to know about my activities and what was happening outside her nursing home. Remember to keep your responses brief and turn the conversation around. You are not the focus.

Exercise

If you are having a challenging time connecting with someone, you might think of a relative or close friend of whom you are fond. How do you treat that individual? What is your interaction like with them? One nursing home aide told me, "I treat everyone like my grandmother, and just love them."

#7 Have a beginner's mind: Ask, don't assume

Assumptions are speculation—not definitive—and often they may be incorrect. I've heard this admonition more than once: "Do not assume." Remember the staff person who assumed the grief-stricken family of atheists wanted clergy and prayers? Both staff and chaplain were embarrassed and the family was angry over the unnecessary intrusion and the added grief. Don't assume, even with the best of intentions. You may very well be very wrong.

Don't assume you know best or know what someone wants or how someone else is feeling. Don't assume the person dying cannot accomplish a task. When we step in, we may cause anger and diminish one's dignity. In time, the one dying will not be able to manage even small movements. For now, permit him to do what he can while he is able.

Do notice. Be like Curious George, or adopt a Buddhist's beginner's mind. This approach encourages our openness to discovery about another. Not "I'm moving this photograph that keeps falling" but rather "I notice this photograph falls. Would you like me to stand it up or move it?" You may learn how special the photo is and why it needs to be nearby despite its current precarious position. The conversation then may focus on how to keep the photo stable while remaining accessible.

Be curious and become a beginner. Curiosity and learning lead us to a lighthearted place, eager to find out about someone else—their desires, hopes, and challenges. With this attitude, we recognize that desires may have changed, so that what was good yesterday isn't good today. Each moment is new. To meet another's needs, we notice, and always ask rather than assume.

#8 Don't initiate touch—but it depends

Your personal relationship will dictate the degree of your physical closeness. For family or close friends, continue to offer connection as you have in the past: a hug, a kiss, holding hands. Even here, be alert to changes in your loved one's condition that warrant a different response. Is someone in pain, or on oxygen? Does the person have thinning skin that bruises easily? Is he withdrawing from such closeness? Pay attention and let him lead you.

When you visit or sing for an individual other than a friend or family member, there are important issues of boundaries— that is, how we define our role and interaction in a particular relationship. As a bedside visitor, you are present for a limited amount of time, in a defined, structured role, which is based on the patient's need for support. While you likely feel drawn to this role because of your desire to be of service, how you choose to act as a result of your feelings is a separate issue. The general rule is not to initiate touch.

But it depends—as my experience with my aunt illustrates. She was at home, in her own bedroom. On this day as I sat with her, she asked me to move her. She complained of discomfort on her left side. "I'm not trained. I might hurt you," I told her. She looked at me intently with her big brown eyes and said, "I trust you, Linda. Please help me." No health aide was available. How could I refuse? I told her what I would do before I did it. As gently as I could, I moved her and she relaxed into the new position.

My interaction with Susan was different. Hospice care referred us to Susan. She was a slight, white-haired lady who enjoyed having her nails painted bright colors. She had a twinkle in her eye, a ready laugh, and a mischievous spirit. From our first encounter, Susan welcomed our visits with much warmth and banter. She sang along when she could, she was interested to know what we'd been up to, and she often told us we made her feel so good.

Susan reached out to us; she wanted a physical connection. She stretched out her arms and took hold of our hands. It's OK, I realized, because she initiated that. At a later visit, she grabbed the front of my sweater, pulled me down with a strength I did not know she had, and kissed me on the cheek.

The months passed. Susan was off hospice, and then back on. During this time, I occasionally sang with a different partner. Others noticed Susan's connection to me in particular. As one person observed, "You seem to give her something she wants and needs." Susan would stare intently at me, with shining eyes and a wide smile. And I held and returned her gaze.

Humans need physical touch. Some psychologists call this need for physical human contact "skin hunger" or "touch hunger." Studies show that simple touch, like a pat on the arm or holding hands, is received as a sign of safety, trust, and compassion. In today's climate, however, a patient's need for simple touch must be carefully weighed within appropriate boundaries. If your visits take you to residential facilities, or you work with hospice or another program, you likely will receive training that addresses touch, boundaries, and other aspects of patient interaction.

Note: While this book focuses on non-medical support modalities, you may wish to be trained to offer hands-on care to your loved one. Ask a nurse or other health care provider to show you, for example, how to turn someone in bed, how to safely move a person to a wheelchair or commode, or how to correctly administer medications.

#9 Leave in peace

Like the showbiz motto "leave 'em laughing," intend to leave someone in a better state than the one before your encounter. In short, aim for the person and family to be relieved that you came—entering their experience, calming their anxieties, and lifting their spirits. Aim to leave them at peace. And if you leave 'em laughing, too, that's just fine.

#10 Just your presence

You are the common denominator in all these guidelines. The principles revolve around you. You are the most important ingredient—you and your presence.

You are more than just presence—like the soup Christine made for her dying author-client in Australia was more than just soup. Indeed, Christine described making just soup for Alistair as "profound."

Someone else may cook just soup, but not you. When you are fixing it for a loved one, you are preparing so much more. Remember *Like Water for Chocolate*? You add very special, even precious, ingredients along with the veggies and the broth. You add your reminiscences of the people around the table on the many occasions at which this dish was greeted with "yum" or "delicious," perhaps even "simply superb" or "my favorite!" Your mind wanders to how you came by the recipe and when you first served it. Perhaps you remember with a smile the variations that worked and the ones that were, well, not repeated. And how quickly it became a household staple, happily consumed both at large festive gatherings and quiet times with just the two of you.

Today, you are making it again. Will it be the last time you enjoy it together? You don't know. But you add an extra dash of gratitude, a tablespoon of joy, a drop or two of tears, and love by the cupful. You stir. You taste. Almost perfect... except it won't last forever.

At a bedside, you, too, offer more—much more than just your presence. *You* are the most important ingredient. You cared enough to be there.

CHAPTER 7

What You Can Actually do to Help the One Dying (and the Family, too)

See your relationship as a place that you go to give,
and not a place that you go to take.
—*Tony Robbins, author and motivational speaker*

You actually can do a great deal. Much is of the "no skills required" variety, although some is better provided by trained hands—training which you could pick up easily if you wish. You'll know where you fit. Some suggestions come into play as a person's health changes. No doubt you will learn of other possibilities, specific to the individual situation, as you enter the intimate experience of that person's end-of-life journey.

Here's a to-do list of welcome actions which are generally appropriate at any time from diagnosis to death. Of course, your approach will differ depending upon your relationship to the person who is dying.

Stay in touch—and give them space

This may be the most important action you can take—to stay in touch—not only with the one dying, but also with the caregiver and family. Everyone wants to feel supported—to know that help and a sympathetic ear are available, just in case. Too many feel left out and abandoned once they become ill. They may view the isolation as a sign that they are no longer valued by others, and not deserving of even a moment.

Please make space in your active, healthy day for a moment—or more. Pick up the phone, or send a card or letter. Let them know you have not forgotten them. Let them know you are available (if indeed you are). Cards? Avoid the get-well ones; they know they are dying. Ask not "how are you doing?" but rather "how are you doing today?" They may not know how they are doing, but they can share what they are feeling today, to navigate the seemingly treacherous waters in which they find themselves.

Visit. A distraught husband was getting groceries when he encountered some women who had been friends of his wife. The women solemnly told him they were praying for her. Exasperated, he yelled, "She needs *you*, not just your prayers!" Keep up your friendships.

Visit—at a time convenient for them. Schedules can be overwhelming; caregivers need a respite; and some semblance of daily life also needs attention. (You can help with all of that, too.) When seeing someone in a facility, you'll need to plan around the care and meal schedule. You'll also need to be considerate of other visitors who arrive unexpectedly. Remember why you are there and calmly and warmly accommodate all comers. And know when it is time for you to leave.

If you are a member of a group—whether sharing, congregational, book club, or choir—confer with the other members to see how they, too, may contribute. Perhaps you'll take turns staying in touch. Perhaps you'll be creative in how to keep him connected and participating as he is able. You can change your gathering location to be with your member in his new circumstances. (I can hear you now. "That's so inconvenient." Yeah. So's dying.)

There are choirs who convene a rehearsal at the person's home or at the facility. Later they may visit and sing at bedside when one of their members is dying. Part of a prayer chain? Keep him on the chain; he can pray wherever he is, even with his current challenges. If you plan outings, consider what minimal alterations may enable him to be present. For example, each family who hosts our annual block party ensures a wheelchair-accessible space so everyone can enjoy the fun, food, and fellowship.

There is also the gift of space, when any connection is too much. When alone time or precious private together time must be preserved. And when you are again welcomed in, and words fail, there may be music and song or the simplicity of a shared silence. All this is possible when you come to be with another.

The challenge for you is not the start, but the keep-going phase. Dying is often a marathon, not a sprint. You may become tired or resentful; you may crave something new and different. You can bet the person dying would like something new and different too—especially a new healthy body and a different outcome. He must stay the course; will you?

People who are dying live in a world of shifting landscapes and unwanted change. They see their friends change and act differently, then even avoid them. They long for steadfast connection. The courage to care includes the stamina to stay in touch for the duration.

A cornucopia of practical, everyday tasks

There is much you can do to ease this time of challenge and transition. There are groceries to be purchased, meals to be made, laundry to be done, errands to run, play dates for the children, transportation to give, notes to be written, cards to be sent, pictures to create, stories to tell. There are medications to manage, and medical appointments to schedule. There are visitors to coordinate, and health-related instructions to record. Pets need care and walking. Add lawn care, gardening, leaf-raking and snow-shoveling. There is laughter, and jokes to tell, and funny movies to watch. There are silly songs to be sung, and books to read aloud. You can clean windows, take the car for service, or offer to fill in so the caregiver has a respite and can go out. See if you can help in some meaningful way in connection with the social, religious, and fraternal organizations to which the family belongs.

Trust the person who is asking how she can help, and tell her what you need. What do you need now, later today, tomorrow? Is it an ongoing need or a specific for-now request? Louis recently reminded me it may not be easy to respond in the moment. When I asked him what his challenges were with his aging, ill parents, he replied, "I'm a bit traumatized because I am in the middle of it and my brain is not thinking as clearly as it usually does." I recalled how our brain can freeze when we are stressed. But after we take several deep breaths, center, and calm ourselves, our more-relaxed mind can process information better. A list of ongoing tasks can be a good reference when receiving an offer of assistance.

Choose to do what works for you and for the family. Add to the list based on what you observe. State specifically what you will do and when. Do not say, "Let me know if you need anything." Do say, "I'd love to bring dinner on Thursday. Does meatloaf sound good? Or what else sounds better? And when I come, I'll take Rover for a walk." Then, do what you say you will do.

Laughter lightens the spirit
Remember that ill and dying people enjoy laughter and lightness as much as anyone. Patch Adams was known for his bulbous red rubber nose that he wore to bring smiles and laughter to the faces of his pediatric patients. He knew his audience, and believed there is truth to "laughter being the best medicine." Norman Cousins, too, used "laughter therapy" to recover from cancer, and often wrote about the effect of positive emotions on health.

Laughter relieves tension and anxiety. In Pennsylvania, a clown transformed our somber mood. When my husband was in the hospital for the last period of time, a clown appeared at the door. We enjoyed many gimmick-inspired guffaws. I remember one in particular because I kept the one-inch wooden cube she gave us. Why this small block? She explained that when Lloyd put it on the floor, as sick as he was, he could still say that he was able to "walk around the block."

Then there was Mary. I met Mary in Connecticut. She was proud of a hooked wall hanging which she had designed to recognize and honor each person who worked at a rehabilitation facility. Mary had been a volunteer there. She described the hanging, and where it was located, and suggested I go see it. I did just that, and we chatted about it afterward. Mary's face lit up as she told me about her craft group. Then she laughed, saying, "We call ourselves The Hookers [double entendre noted] because we gather together to work on latch hook projects." More laughter. Those Hookers were a loyal group, visiting and supporting Mary throughout her last months.

At another facility, I visited Joan. Her door was closed so I knocked, opened it slowly, poked my head in, and called out a hello. (Closed doors may mean a resident is receiving personal care or a medical treatment that requires privacy.) Both Joan and her roommate were awake and dressed. I asked if I could enter. Joan was having a breathing treatment, hence the closed door. As I sat down, I grinned, and my smile grew wider. I said what came to mind. "You know Joan, with that mask over your face I could say anything to you right now and you couldn't talk back." It was great to hear her hearty laugh despite the oxygen mask on her face.

Bring sunshine and lightness with you. I wear a big smile and offer it freely and genuinely. It puts people at ease. It may bring smiles to their faces. It makes me feel good, which makes them feel good, which makes me feel good that they are feeling better than they were. It's a wonderful circular cycle of goodness to participate in!

Hard work: conversations and reconciliation

There are conversations that, while difficult and painful, hold out the hope of reconciliation and completion. Having these talks, including ones with family that address personal and spiritual matters, benefit both the dying and their family, according to Dr. Ira Byock. In *Dying Well: Peace and possibilities at the end of life*, he writes that patients died more "peacefully and families felt enriched" for having engaged in these deep, heartfelt exchanges.

It is better to hold conversations when the person dying is alert and lucid. Such a talk might be challenging to initiate. Many sources are available to give you the words. The Conversation Project is one. Talking about death over dinner is another. Your role may be to initiate, arrange for, record or support a heartfelt dialogue.

Planning-for-death talks

When the reality of death is accepted, the time may be right to ask the person dying what he wants his dying to look like. Working together, you may outline a bucket list of yet-to-do activities as well as a plan for his remaining days as death nears. Plans may include where to die, who is present, whether music or other modalities are desired, and so forth. Conversations might detail whether a funeral or memorial service or other event is desired as well as burial arrangements.

If any of the important end-of-life health forms—including advanced directive, health care proxy, do-not-resuscitate orders, power of attorney—remain incomplete (see the Appendices for a list), this is the time to have a serious discussion with family and with physicians, as appropriate to your relationship with the dear one who is dying. (If there is no will, that's another item in need of attention.)

Hoped-for reconciliation talks

The dying may wish to reach out to repair strained relationships. You might assist in the effort by locating or contacting the individual, or holding the telephone or writing letters dictated to you when strength begins to wane. These are hopeful—and anxious—entreaties which may be rejected. When they are, you might suggest practices—such as meditation, guided visualizations, burnt offerings of letters or Ho'oponopono—by which the dying may yet achieve a sense of resolution and peace.

Exercise

I learned Ho'oponopono (pronounced ho-oh-po-no-po-no) decades ago in this form:

Say the name of the person to whom it is directed, and then say: "I love you. Please forgive me for my part. I am sorry. Thank you." To make things right, energetically, say it at anytime in your life for anyone. Why not think of someone now? Call up the circumstances and your feelings, and then offer this prayer. It will begin to clear out and clean the energy around you and this person.

Projects to complete a life

In nearing the close of our life, reviewing it, creating legacy projects that outlive us, and attending to our material possessions, all offer us opportunities to highlight our achievements and the meaning we take from the way we lived. You might assist with any of these.

Life review

It is said that we live our lives forward but understand them backward. Looking backward, we gain a sense of pride and achievement at all we have done and been, even with the inevitable detours and disappointments. Having dredged up forgotten tales of a long-ago life, we may be eager to pass on these stories to a new generation, sharing them with family and friends. On one visit, we tape-recorded an uncle who shared the story of his early years in an orphanage and then a series of foster homes before enlisting in the Army, completing college, and creating a life as a mining engineer and business consultant. You might interview your relative or friend.

There are also public initiatives to preserve family stories. Some towns have their own program to record audio or video of local residents who can paint a historical picture of a changing life through the years. One national initiative is StoryCorps. Its mission is to preserve and share humanity's stories from people of all backgrounds and beliefs. Now, as life ebbs, we may feel a deep appreciation and gratitude for our own life— and for life itself. What a place of contentment to be in as we complete our time here.

Legacy projects

Some legacy work creates a record of the life of the dying person, through stories, pictures, or special objects. Suggestions come in many shapes and sizes, from family reunions and scrapbooks to ethical wills and boxes of cherished recipes. A young mother of two boys, ages two and five, made videotapes paired with small gifts for each year up to their 18th birthday. My mother made quilts for each of her grandchildren, completing the last quilt for my then nine-month-old son before she died.

Paula Wrenn and Jo Gustely's *Dying Well with Hospice: a compassionate guide to end of life care* describes a slice-of-life celebration. Held before death, the host invites attendees to bring photos and pose for photos, record their memories in a journal, display other memorabilia, create a scrapbook highlighting the interests of the dying guest of honor—and do it all while enjoying slices of pie. Over the next days, the person dying can look through and read these loving messages—or have them read to him. After death, a treasured family keepsake remains.

Other legacy projects are as imaginative as their participants. David Giffels worked with his father designing and building his father's coffin. Some families choose to film their loved one's final moments. Others may copy and keep the playlist of special songs chosen to be played during the final days. Then there are community-benefitting memorials. One might establish a scholarship fund, start a foundation, or launch a series of programs to benefit the community. One such legacy might be to collect and distribute food donations to a variety of local organizations.

Possessions: reflection and disposition

I have given away a number of personal items and culled through other stuff over the last few years. I don't anticipate an early death—although one never knows—but I am aware of all the little things that tend to accumulate during the passage of time. What calls up a particular sadness for me are those precious-to-me items which will never hold the same degree of honor and joy in anyone else's life. I can see myself wanting to physically hold and remember everything about them one last time. Perhaps this kind of reflection would offer you some solace and closure, too.

Disposal of possessions is another issue altogether. Take one cursory glance at all the various and numerous possessions and it is a daunting task. No wonder we often give up, don't try, and leave it for anyone else to clean up and clear out after we're gone.

Then again, we might choose those items which we would love to see cherished by someone else. Or we could ask family what, if anything, they would wish to have as a keepsake.

You might help by tagging items with the name of its future owner. You might arrange a give-away, now, while the giver can enjoy the satisfaction of personally passing along treasured items. (When you are a recipient, receive your remembrance graciously, even though the item may not hold the same value and meaning to you.) You could write descriptions and the history of each item and why they meant so much. Your help will be cheerfully welcomed by some. For others, clearing and working through items that hold emotional attachment is a solitary endeavor.

Personal care—or not

Grooming, re-positioning, transferring from one place to another, bathing, feeding. As our abilities gradually diminish, others must do for us what we can no longer do for ourselves. Although these services more often are provided by someone trained in personal care, as a family member you, too, could be instructed regarding these tasks so as not to injure your loved one. Even without training, there may be exceptional circumstances under which you might offer a hand—literally and figuratively.

Uncle Paul was actually my dad's uncle, a widower with no children. When I returned to graduate school nearby, I visited Paul regularly. We shared thoughtful conversations, went for drives and I showed him how to cook asparagus. Now he was in the nursing wing of a New Jersey hospital.

Uncle Paul brightened as he saw me. He was alert and sitting up with one of those movable tray stands across his bed. I opened my laptop computer, placed it on the tray and regaled him with stories and pictures. As we finished, I noticed single-serving pudding cups on a shelf along the wall. I mentioned them and he reminded me how much he enjoyed them.

"Would you like one?"

"Yes, if it isn't too much trouble."

I tore off the protective seal, found a spoon, removed my laptop and deposited the treat in its place. As Uncle Paul raised his hands from beneath the tray, I noticed he, like his older sister, suffered from chronic arthritis, which had transformed his fingers into rigid, unmovable appendages. Someone would need to feed him in a way that would feel good.

"So, Uncle Paul, how about you taking a taste?" I picked up the spoon, scooped up a bit of pudding, and offered it to him.

"Hmm. Now that's good," he said as a smile spread across his crinkly face.

I thought about how as infants others must do everything for us—hopefully doing so without resentment or embarrassment, and with love and tenderness. I realized that at the end of life, we're in a similar situation, needing someone to keep us clean and comfortable. May we now give, with reverence and compassion, what we received in our earlier need.

Living fully, living normally, while dying

Live fully while you are dying. Aim for normalcy within the circumstances. As one person admonished his family, "I'm not dead yet!" Avoid pity, gloom, and tiptoeing around. Invite jokes, sass, and sun. Yes, there are extra visitors coming and going, but as much as possible be together as you have been.

Enjoy ordinary routines—from morning coffee to strolls and family get-togethers. Take little outings, enjoy physical closeness, walk the beach, sit under the stars. Reminisce about cherished moments from your shared life. With modifications, you may continue to take pleasure in shared activities. Treasure each and every one. Later, when the person is no longer able to communicate but remains alert, you may do the talking, share music, read aloud, or simply offer your gentle, loving presence. Live fully and joyfully each precious moment. You do not know when this moment will be the last.

CHAPTER 8

What to do as You Keep Watch and Death Nears

We cannot follow you where you are going,
What you are feeling, we cannot know.
But we will keep watch...
'til your journey brings you home.
—Becky Reardon, songwriter

"Don't worry, Dad. Just talk to Joe and tell him what you've been doing."

And then I walked outside, leaving my dad at the bedside of his long-time friend.

Dad couldn't drive after his stroke. That was probably the worst outcome he could have imagined. I became his driver and made time to bring him for visits to his old and dear friends who lived at a distance—visits that likely would be the last.

This day I left my home in New York State and picked him up in central Pennsylvania. We were traveling to New Jersey with the intention of seeing Tillie, who had been my mom's maid of honor, and her husband Joe, who was a baker. They had owned a bakery and I had fond memories of traveling home with bags of baked goods after one of our family visits.

We arrived at their door and found no one home. I located a phone number for one of their sons and learned from him that his mom was in the hospital and his dad was in a facility, dying. A long-time smoker, Tillie was on oxygen and herself getting closer to death, but as she described her husband's condition, it was clear he would go first. She provided the address and we left. We knew Joe had had some health challenges but had not expected to find him in skilled nursing care.

After stopping and asking for directions—no smartphones yet—I navigated the 20-minute drive and pulled into the parking area. I opened the trunk and took out Dad's walker. I opened his door and offered a hand, then my arm, to help him from the car. We slowly made our way to the entrance.

Stopping in the lobby, we inquired after Joe. We proceeded through the hallways and approached him. I was startled to witness his small, contracted frame, which appeared to be overpowered by the size of the bed. The light from the nearby window illuminated the peaceful area. The bed was set in an open space without enclosures—no door, additional furniture, or even, thankfully, the intrusive noise of a 24/7 television.

I noticed that my dad hung back. It was up to me to take the lead. I drew close to Joe, somewhat leaning over the bed, and clearly and slowly said, "Hi Joe. It is good to see you. I'm Linda, and my dad—Al—is here to say hi."

Joe opened his eyes. He slowly turned his head. Softly we heard, "Al. Hey, it's good to see you."

I brought a chair and placed it at the bedside. "Why don't you sit down, Dad?" He sat and I stood for some moments in silence, both of us looking at Joe.

Then I spoke. I let Joe know that we had visited his wife. I told him that I had been in touch with his daughter over the years. I told him I remembered his long hours and hard work providing for his family. I told him I so enjoyed his baked goodies. I told him I appreciated the good, long friendship he had had with my folks.

Joe listened. The cookies-and-cakes remark brought a slight smile to his face.

I paused. I told Joe I would give him time with Dad, and I would go outside for a few minutes. I told him I would return to say goodbye.

I looked at my dad. He seemed uncomfortable. Indeed, I felt he really wanted to leave with me.

He looked up at me. "What could I talk about?"

"Why not just tell Joe how it's going with you, what you're up to these days. Maybe what you remember about the old days with Joe and Tillie." Then I turned away.

It wasn't as though my dad had never faced death. He cared for my mom on home hospice until she died. He enlisted at age 17, and as a Navy man and Seabee he would be sent to Iwo Jima. He never talked about those years. Well, not to me. When Dad was in declining health but still mobile, I would bring him, albeit with difficulty, to the house for special occasions. He and my husband would remain at the dining table and talk about the war. Later I Googled *Iwo Jima* and discovered that only 25 percent of the U.S. soldiers returned from that island conflict. My dad was one of the fortunate few.

As I waited outside, I wondered whether my dad was seeing himself in that bed in not too long of a time. I wondered whether they were talking or resting in silence. Either would be good; just being a quiet, caring presence is in and of itself a precious gift to give.

I returned in perhaps ten minutes. I was sensitive to my dad's anxiety about feeling unprepared for the position I had put him in. (From this distance, I realize that his situation then mirrored mine in that earlier hospital ward. I, at least, had suggested conversation starters.)

We said our goodbyes to Joe, grateful we had made the trip. Joe died two weeks later. His wife followed soon after.

You never know when the last time will be. I was scheduled to visit my dear friend Marian but could not reach her to confirm my arrival date. When I called her apartment, a strange voice answered. One of her daughters told me Marian was out of the hospital and now in rehab following a stroke.

I had met Marian almost ten years earlier when I joined her ADORE (A Dialogue On Race and Ethnicity) group. We were also in a book group together. When she moved away, we kept in touch and I visited whenever my travels took me anywhere near her. Having retired from a career as a registered nurse specializing in psychiatric/mental health nursing and hospice, Marian was thrilled and supportive when I began my work with the dying. And I was thrilled and supportive of her writing endeavors, especially happy upon the publication of her chapbook, *Unicorn in Captivity*, in which she explored themes of racial and social justice.

Right then I decided to make the trip from Massachusetts to Pennsylvania. I felt I had to see her right away. We talked, she rested, I sang. I told her I'd return in a few weeks' time following an already-scheduled trip. I was glad I had visited; Marian died before I could return.

Betty, who worked both at a nursing home and in hospice care, reports that she's heard survivor regret "more than anything." She explained:

> So many people live with regret, saying, *Why didn't I go see this person?* You just don't know. And maybe at the end of it too you can kind of be at peace with yourself, knowing you made the effort and knowing you got the sense or the feeling that OK, there is something after this life. Maybe it will help you at your end, too.

Make the time and connect

It's not always easy to be in touch. Sometimes, guilt is a huge deterrent, as it was for a woman with whom I had a truncated exchange at a conference. She admitted, reluctantly, that she does not visit family or friends, even though they are ill, because she feels guilty for being out of touch. Therefore, she maintains her distance. Before I could continue the conversation, she abruptly turned and walked away. Sadly, her guilt and separation, unaddressed, may continue to haunt her.

Martin's son, David, suggests this perspective to help overcome hesitancy to reach out:

> It's not about *you*. *I* don't know what to say. *I* don't know what to do. Those are all about *me*, as opposed to *What does that person need? How can I be a support?*
>
> I gained a greater appreciation for my dad—who he was, and all he did. Before my parents died, I told them I loved them.
>
> At bedside, there's a metaphysical—a spiritual—level of communication that is something beyond what I would consider comprehensible communication. There's a knowing you can't explain.

Particularly when it means traveling a distance, we may hesitate to plan time together. But if we are alert and listen closely, we may decide to clear our calendar, make the journey, and in hindsight be grateful we did. After multiple calls from his brother, Gary rearranged his schedule and flew to Honolulu on a Wednesday:

> [My older brother John] never told me he had been on the liver transplant list for two years. His

son Greg, my nephew, only found out when he took his dad to the hospital and heard it from the doctor.

Thursday and Friday we all went to the Hawaii State Baseball Games. After the last game, my brother was back in the hospital. Greg and I sat with him for hours. When he woke up, he insisted on going home, over the doctor's objections. Big Bro kept saying he was fine, wanted food, and talked about life, and much more.

Greg came over Saturday afternoon. We ate our favorite foods and watched my brother's favorite *Star Wars* and *Star Trek* movies until late into the night. We had a great time!

Sunday, my brother asked me to go to the store and refused to come along for the ride. After I left the house, I called Greg and asked him to check on his dad.

Two hours later, Greg called saying his dad was incoherent, had fallen and couldn't get up. John was taken to the hospital, did not regain consciousness and crossed over peacefully in his sleep. My Big Bro John had completed his Earth mission and had graduated Earth School.

When we heed a call, we put the needs of someone else first. Acting sooner rather than later, we may be able to grab the last opportunity to say goodbye in person. Gary listened, and has no regrets.

Even with good intentions, we may not be at the bedside. Perhaps a rapidly progressing medical condition or a sudden, unexpected death is the cause. Sometimes personal circumstances of family, responsibilities, and geographical distance keep us away, or delay our departure until it is too late. Sometimes unusual circumstances, like a pandemic, intervene. And sometimes, we are there, but step out of the room or look at our phone, and miss the last breath. The cause of our absence and how we feel about it—as well as who died and how they died—all influence the depth and length of our grief and mourning.

Say what you need to say

In this dying time, there's an urgency to say what you need to say—about grievances and about gratitude. The specter of death can stir up unhealed estrangements, childhood hurts, and unanswered questions only this person can answer. Hearts may be full, too, with gratitude and with grief at the impending absence of this beloved person from your life. Talking from the heart is not easy for everyone. How do we say it?

Exercise

What do you want your memory of this person, of this relationship, to be? For this is the essence of this moment for you and the other.

Take a few deep breaths, quiet yourself, and close your eyes. If you were a movie director—and you can and do direct your own life—how would you write this final scene?

Knowing the parting you wish, how do you make it happen? We cannot control another's actions, but we do control our own. I summoned my courage and found reconciliation and completion with my mom. I am at peace that this is my enduring memory of her.

Perhaps we had a typical mother-daughter push-and-pull relationship. Perhaps ours was exacerbated by her needing to work full-time and therefore my needing to be an adult before my time—having dinner on the table for the family, being a latch-key kid with an unruly sibling, being on my own a great deal of the time. Later, I worked, took out loans and paid my own way through college and graduate school. After graduation I left the state, and essentially eloped; until I had a child seven years later, I don't remember a whole lot of keeping in touch.

Then Mom was diagnosed with colon cancer. She was embarrassed and distraught about dealing with the colostomy bag and so asked to have it surgically reversed. Her slide toward death quickened. She did live to see and spend time with all her grandchildren during the following years. She died at age 63 when my son, my fourth and last child, was nine months old.

During those last months, I visited more frequently. Once with my infant son. The next trip with him and his two-and-a-half-year-old sister. I went alone on the final visit. I was in my art phase then, so I'd brought along my sketch pad. Mom had wasted away, skin over bones, and I could not bring myself to draw her. I sat with her and asked about her life and any regrets she may have had. We prayed the 23rd Psalm, which was her favorite, and which I had memorized as part of my Sunday School education.

I remember our standing together. I remember that I gently hugged her. I see myself stepping back, holding her at arm's length, looking into her eyes and saying, "I know we haven't always gotten along. I'm so sorry for my part, for anything I ever said, did, or didn't do. When we meet again, I hope we do it better next time. I love you."

And for the first time in my life, I heard Mom telling me, "I love you, too." I flew home. She went into a coma and died two weeks later.

For me, it wasn't about who was right or wrong. It wasn't about who coulda, shoulda, woulda done this or that. I took the step—for her and for me. I knew this would be the last opportunity to make things right between us, and so I found the courage to create the best ending I could create.

So here's your mom, dad, or friend, and you want to say something from your heart—but it isn't easy, and sometimes you just can't find the words. An aide tells this story of one of her patients:

> Edwin had been in hospice for months. When I visited him, he told me stories and we would talk. His two sons would pop in every now and then. They appeared to take comfort from knowing that I took extra time with their dad. They did not spend extra time. They'd pop in, bring junk food, wouldn't stay and chat, or even just sit for a while.

KEEPING WATCH AS DEATH NEARS   127

Walt found it easy. He was older and firmly believed in the continuation of life after death. Reflecting on his time at his father's bedside, Walt offered these observations:

> I think a lot of people felt it was weird for me to say to my dad, "Are you ready to die? Are you ready to pass? Is there anything we could talk about that would help you?" That type of thing. But he was dying. He knew he was dying. So avoiding the subject—I didn't see any sense in that. My brothers were there, too, and sat with Dad. They could not talk to him.
>
> So when you mentioned the title of your book it impressed me so much. That caught my heart. Because I never knew that before, but that was exactly the difference between me and everybody else. I had the courage to step forward and care about what he was going through, not what *I* was going through. And that was why I received a blessing.

What you might say

Talk *to* your loved one, not *about* him. Talk as you would if he were sitting across the table from you. Say, *I remember when…* or *You taught me…* or *I'm sorry about…* or *I never told you…* or *Thank you for…* or *I love you.* Tell him: *I will miss you and I will be sad. But you have my permission to go; don't worry because I will be all right.*

You might recall shared memories. Silly stories. Heartfelt ones. Songs that were sung—and then sing a few bars.

Offer simple words of consolation and comfort. *You are safe. You are loved. We will remember you. You lived a good life. You are not alone. Rest easy.* In the quiet of the moment, see your heart open and overflowing with unconditional love and peace toward this person whom you will not again see in the flesh.

Create a sanctuary

A serene space enhances our dying experience. Even when we are nonresponsive as we edge closer to transition, our unconscious registers what is occurring—sounds, smells, and movements—in our surroundings. This is why we sing and talk to a sleeping person. It is also why we create an environment of tranquility, whether at home or in a facility.

Some facilities have created private rooms for persons nearing death. You may request that your loved one be moved there. Ask if you are free to bring objects, music, and other items to personalize the space.

Let your earlier-completed written plan guide you. If you were unable to have that conversation, choose from these options—and others you may know—to create a calm environment that honors the sanctity of the upcoming passage.

- ✓ Flowers, plants, dimmed lighting or candles (no candles around oxygen usage).
- ✓ Pictures, photos, drawings by children or grandchildren; sacred objects/altar.
- ✓ Read aloud from spiritual texts, special poems or writings; recite familiar prayers.

✓ Sing, play music or use other modalities appropriate to your culture, values, and beliefs. *Options include*: aromatherapy, incense, massage, guided meditation, dreamwork, therapeutic touch, art, Kirtan Hindu chants, Gregorian or Taize singing, and Threshold Choir songs. All relax the body and mind, and open the spirit to the mystery that awaits.

✓ Hold a phone or iPad close so distant relatives or friends can offer their goodbyes.

✓ Offer gentle touch: hold hands, touch feet, arms. Some children and spouses climb into the bed; it's what you're comfortable with and what you feel called to do.

✓ Clergy visitation for prayers, blessings, and rites for the dying.

✓ Hold your own ritual or prayer service. *For example*: when I saw the many out-of-town relatives who had gathered around the bed of the woman who was their mother, mother-in-law, grandmother, and aunt, I led an impromptu vesper service. We prayed and gave thanks for the life of the one who lay before us. She passed peacefully the following morning.

✓ If you wish, you may limit visitors to family only. You also may request that medical staff refrain from entering the room.

Your aim is to create a calm, harmonious environment of deep peace, of celebration and of remembrance. Laugh and cry, and keep the focus on the one in the bed, offering encouraging and loving words of thanks, of reconciliation, and of permission for the letting go. May you do it all in a way that honors the spirit and personality of the one before you.

Keeping vigil: the final watch

Stay with me, remain here with me, watch and pray. The words, based on the Gospel of Matthew, call us to the bedside. The words call us to be present, to notice, and yes, even to wonder at the mystery unfolding before us. The words become a call from the one dying.

Once someone is determined to be actively dying (described in Chapter 2), vigil begins. This is the final watching and waiting that may last from a few hours to a few days. Because "we know neither the day nor the hour," we often keep vigil around the clock, determined to be present at the moment of death.

I have sat at bedsides and kept vigil. This is Kathy's story:

I knock and enter the semi-private room and notice her husband sitting on the window side of her bed at the far end of the room. I had met him before. I greet Kathy—and every patient—whether or not they appear alert. Kathy is quiet and unresponsive. Such a change since I last saw her. Her skin has a noticeable gray pallor.

I greet her husband Robert and mention that hospice notified me of Kathy's changed condition. I ask his permission to stay and sing. Even though a family requests bedside singing, if at any time they wish private alone time, I respect their decision and leave.

Robert welcomes my presence. He wants to talk, and launches into a story. Two days ago, he says, he wheeled his wife into the activity room to hear a music program. At one of the songs, he proudly reports, she began singing along—this from someone who had long ago ceased talking. Next he described his wife's enjoyment of bananas, and that he brings some mashed when he visits. This last time he was surprised and delighted when Kathy clearly said *banana*.

Then he turned to what was on his heart. "Every morning I sing our song. But I haven't yet."

I looked at the wall clock. "There are ten minutes remaining to the morning." I encouraged him.

"All right, then." He picked up his smartphone and fiddled to find the song. "I've been singing this song every morning since we married, but I like to hear it while I'm singing. It helps me with the tune. I'm not really a very good singer."

He leaned forward from his sitting position, held the phone close to his wife and pushed play. He gently stroked her arm as he sang along to the music, *When I saw you standing there / I 'bout fell out my chair....* He made it to the last refrain of Lobo's song before he began crying.

I wondered how I ought to respond. I didn't know the song well, but I knew the chorus. Should I sing?

Would he feel I was intruding on their song if I did? After another moment of hesitation I began, quietly, and finished the song. He thanked me for jumping in, and I was grateful he was not upset.

"I'm sure Kathy loved hearing the song you two shared. Why don't I leave so you have private time to spend with her?" I rose and said goodbye to both of them. As I walked to my car, I kept hearing *seven o'clock* in my head. I decided to return around seven that evening.

It was 7:20 when I arrived. I've read about persons near death displaying glowing faces—and in this moment I see it. Kathy looked radiant, nothing like her earlier countenance. I actually caught my breath when I saw her.

I wedged my collapsible camp chair into the narrow space between the bedrail and the indoor heating/cooling unit. It was a tight fit and I was a bit uncomfortable but it would work. I was out of the staff's way and at Kathy's side.

I again greeted her and then sat in silence. When I felt ready, I sang. *You are loved, deeply loved.... Dear one...thank you for all you have done...all you have given.... Your soul knows the way to take you home today.* Songs punctuated with sacred silence.

A nurse came in to check on her and stayed for a bit. I noticed tears running down the nurse's cheeks. "The words and the melody are so beautiful," she commented. An aide entered, turned around, and then waited in the doorway until the end of a song. "Well, that sure satisfied my soul!" she exclaimed before disappearing into the hallway.

Kathy's breathing slowed, the span between each breath lengthening. The nurse returned with another, each took one of Kathy's hands, and waited only a few minutes until she took her last breath. I sang *Be at Peace* as a benediction, and left. I was grateful to have heeded Spirit's call to return, to be present, and to offer Kathy the parting gift of song.

What might you do during vigil?

You may continue any of the supportive behaviors listed earlier for creating a sanctuary. You'll also want to be mindful of these particular circumstances.

Comfort care and possible bursts of energy: Care includes repositioning and adjusting pillows as needed, moistening lips, cooling a hot forehead with a damp cloth, putting on or taking off bed coverings. If the person appears anxious or in pain, medication, soothing words, or a reassuring touch help. Remember, it is not unusual to see bursts of energy or leg restlessness—as though the person is already walking home.

Care for yourself. Yes, you want to be at bedside. And you need to care for yourself during these hours—or days. You need sleep. You need nourishment. You need support. Perhaps sit in shifts. When breathing changes and death is near, you can be notified.

Leaving the room. Although you may wish to witness the last breath, some of the dying will not or cannot transition unless everyone has left the room. Someone gets a cup of coffee or takes a short walk down the hall—and that's when the person dies. Have we not heard stories like this? In case your loved one needs to be alone, consider leaving the room periodically.

Your interior dialogue. Your presence and your vibrations of peace and comfort—or tension and anxiety—are being received and felt. And more so, now that the one dying is moving more fully into spirit. Martin's son David had talked about a different level of communication, a "knowing I can't explain." Sarah too, "knew" that a dying gentleman was anxious and fearful because he did not know what would happen at death. She mentally offered simple words of instruction and assurance that he would be safe. We might do the same.

Keep your focus here, now. This will be an inner focus more than a physical one. Clear your mind. Think, see, and be peace. You may send love and encouragement. I send supportive energy for the person's highest and best. I need not know what highest and best means for that individual; I trust that whatever best meets their need in the moment will be provided.

You may pray. Using familiar prayers—e.g., the rosary, Scripture, beloved poems—we contemplate their deeper meaning and offer them up for the benefit of this dying soul. Pray for safe passage. Pray for comfort.

You may meditate. Christians call this contemplation or centering prayer; a similar practice by another name. *Tonglen* is a Buddhist practice anyone can use at bedside. If you wish to try it, here is a description:

Exercise—*at bedside*

Begin by settling yourself and focusing on your breath. Notice how the breath moves in… and moves out.… Then with the in breath, we breathe in suffering or discomfort, especially of the one dying. On the out breath, we release the suffering, breathing out kindness, compassion and peace to all, especially to the one dying. As a tree cleans the air by taking in carbon dioxide and releasing life-giving oxygen, we, too, clear the energetic air. Each of us, regardless of how badly we feel, can find some measure of kindness, compassion, and peace to send out to others. Don't forget to include yourself in this.

You may sit in the profound silence. Still mind. Still body. Know that all is well.

Being peaceful, being patient. You are a mere observer, with no power to hurry the unfolding. Be at peace and remain calm. Trust the words of a song I sing that we *can't arrive early and…can't arrive late* at the gate to the next reality. The time will unfold as it is meant to unfold. Be patient. All is well.

"Dying well" and "good death." How someone dies matters. For survivors, the circumstances of the final scene will remain in their memories throughout their lives. For them, it is healing to witness a good death. For the person whose life has ended, dying well encompasses satisfactory resolution and reconciliation as well as an easy, peaceful passing.

Connection. Compassion. Love. Remembrance. Reconciliation. Surely, both the dying and the survivors would take solace from even brief encounters of connection and reconciliation. We can control only ourselves. Can we summon the courage to move toward another? When we do, the deceased will have died well, and for both of us it will have been a good death.

CHAPTER 9

Why Music Holds a Noteworthy Place

For heights and depths no words can reach,
Music is the soul's own speech.
—Author unknown

"I like your hair. Is it always curly?"

The thin, old woman who asked the question sat diagonally from me. As she turned, I noticed her hair was gray-white and very short. She sported attractive spiky curls on top.

"Yes, it is naturally curly," I replied.

"I'm always afraid of letting my hair grow, but I don't like my hair short, either. I have a cowlick and it sticks out. How does it look in the back?"

I reassured her—honestly—that her hair on top and on the back of her head looked wonderful. As I spoke, a song I sing came to mind. And so I went with it and sang, *You are beautiful / Be yourself / After all, everyone else is taken.* She laughed, as did the presenter who had overheard our exchange while waiting for more people to arrive.

I finished the song. *You are beautiful / Be yourself / May your fullness awaken.* She had a smile on her face as she turned to listen to the speaker.

Almost an hour and a half later the gathering ended. The woman swiveled in her seat and asked, "What's that again about being myself?" I repeated the words, speaking them this time. She laughed, and had a huge grin on her face. As she stood to leave she said, "I ought to hang around with you rather than my therapist. I feel great!"

I'm certain you, too, have a selection of music that makes you feel great. From infancy, music is part of us. Our breathing has a rhythm. Our heart has a beat. Our pulse keeps time. Someone sang to you, softly, gently, lovingly. You felt safe, cared for, loved. You were reassured—even though you did not know that big word then—and were able to quiet down and go to sleep. As adults, this magic of music still works on us—body, mind and soul—throughout our living and our dying. We can choose a piece of music that makes us feel the way we wish to feel.

Music as medicine

It would take a fair amount of space to list the research confirming the benefits of music for our physical, emotional, and mental health. Here's a short list of findings.

Music:

- Lessens stress and anxiety
- Reduces depression
- Facilitates emotional release
- Improves one's mood and optimism
- Lessens feelings of isolation and loneliness
- Leads to increased involvement in activities
- Creates bonding experiences
- Opens communication and stimulates conversation
- Fosters happiness and pleasure
- Can facilitate a peaceful death
- Stimulates the brain
- Slows the decline of cognitive skills
- Increases energy levels
- Increases cardiovascular strength
- Strengthens the immune system
- Improves respiratory function

Offering so many benefits for all of us throughout life, it's no wonder music has been called "sonic massage" and "medicine"!

Exercise

Do you have music playing now?

Go ahead and put on a favorite tune—or two—that makes you feel great.

Helping persons with stroke and dementia
Considering this list of improved outcomes, therapists use music with stroke and dementia patients. They are seeing some remarkable results. From Indiana, Judy shares her brother-in-law Raymond's story:

> Although Raymond loved to dance, he especially enjoyed singing. He was always part of singing groups, and led choral groups while in the Navy. He married, fathered five children and then lost his wife. After his remarriage, he had a stroke. He was confined to a wheelchair with one side of his body paralyzed, and could no longer speak. It seemed that singing and the pleasure it brought him were gone from his life.
>
> It seemed like a miracle when one day the family played some music and discovered that Raymond could sing. They would get him singing and his face would light up. Life came back into his face when he was singing. It seemed that he could still find happiness from singing that he did not find from life.

Research shows that Raymond was not alone in his ability to speak in song. Some stroke patients, who are unable to talk, are able to express themselves when they sing what they wish to say.

Music's therapeutic value appears to extend also to dementia patients. The film *Alive Inside* depicts persons who had not spoken in years, but who begin singing when given headphones with playlists of music from their generation. It's as though a switch has been flipped to *on*. For some, the musical breakthrough leads to conversations—at least temporarily. Music does indeed seem to bring people back to life.

And then there's music for the dying

Some of us, while yet healthy, accumulate our own collection of meaningful songs that we wish to hear as we are dying. From Abba to Zydeco, vocal or instrumental, we each have our preferences. Of course, it helps when we tell others, so that when the time comes, our songs will be played.

I was outlining this book project to a couple we visited. Suddenly, Catherine, a physician, clutched her shirt to her heart. With tears beginning to streak her cheeks, she looked intently across the room at her husband and said, "I've never told you, but I have a playlist of songs that I want to hear as I am dying." Unknowingly, I had given her the opening she needed to share this news with her husband.

Better to choose now while you are able. Make and add to your requested music list whenever you hear a tune that is an oh-yeah-*that*-one pick. Whether you create paper- or technology-based lists, be sure to tell your family and friends that a list exists, and where they will find it when it is needed.

Creating such a list can be a fun, shared activity. It was for Jill and her dad. I met Jill at a town gathering. When she asked what I did, I described my writing about music and dying. Instantly, her face lit up:

"Don't you love music? It was such a bonding experience for me when my father was dying. I put his favorite music on my iPod. We talked and shared. Today is the anniversary of his death. His name is Al."

"That's my dad's name, too," I said. "Let's remember both of them."

Following a brief moment of silence, she continued.

"When my playlist circulates and Chet Atkins comes on—which was one of my dad's favorites—I think of Dad, and of how great the music was for us. You know, we always have music on in our home."

Exercise

What type of music or specific songs would you choose to hear as you are nearing your death? It's not too early to begin your list. (I have.)

Music is always heard

When someone is sleeping or nonresponsive, music remains a blessing. When I was new to singing at bedside, I was partnered with someone whose apparent practice was to sing only to alert patients. That did not feel correct to me. I suggested we stay and sing, albeit quietly. And so we did. And I have continued to do so. On occasion, the person may stir or wake up. Just as often, she will sleep through our visit, not knowing we had been there. But while singing, we may notice physical changes in her—for example, deeper or more rhythmic breathing, diminished or a cessation of restlessness, even a deep breath and an audible sigh of release.

Remember that music and song are sound, vibration. Picture the way ripples flow across a pond when you toss in a rock. That's the way vibration flows out when you speak or sing or play music. In one way or another, the vibration is being heard, and it is being received. The vibration is flowing around, caressing your body—all parts of it, not only your physical body but also your emotional, mental, and spiritual body. Here is Margie's story:

Margie wore a flowery top, and she was covered with a nondescript blanket. She listed a bit to her left side. Margie was a new referral, and I had been told she was anxious.

I wondered what she was anxious about. Anxious about being exposed in the hallway, lined up with other residents who were positioned there (they could not ambulate independently)? Anxious about her health? About the stuff of her life? Or anxious about death and dying? After all, this was a hospice referral. Perhaps she was anxious about all of the above.

We opened our camp chairs and sat next to Margie. I looked at her. Her unfocused eyes were flitting around and she was restless. I said hello, introduced myself, and told her that we were there to offer healing songs. I took a breath and closed my eyes. I asked to be present.

For some visits, like today, being present is more challenging. There is the necessary busy-ness of medical staff, the pushing of medication carts through the hall, and our sitting directly across from the nurses' station. Other staff wheeled residents, responded to cries of help, or hurried past us to dispose of the detritus from either cleaning a person or from cleaning a room after someone's death.

So I am present, here, now. Quiet. Peaceful. And I am open to receive songs that will benefit this particular person—Margie—at this particular time, in this particular place. Easy, rest easy, comes to mind. And so we begin. *Easy, rest easy. Let every trouble drift away...love enfolds you and holds you safe.*

As we sing, we watch. We notice that Margie's breathing settles into a regular rhythm. It becomes slower and she makes what sounds and looks like a deep sigh. Her restless movements diminish and then cease. Her eyelids begin to droop. We repeat the song several times, adding harmony. Margie's eyes close and she is still.

We continue quietly. *You are safe in the arms of love...may you rest in the arms of love.* After some silence, we continue. *In the quiet of this moment, I am at peace, all is well.* Before we fold up our chairs and silently steal away, we sing one of my songs, *Be at Peace.*

Three months after I began attending rehearsals of a newly forming Threshold Choir, the first melody and lyric came to me. On that July day, I was sitting in a silent Quaker meeting for worship. Words and music for *The Light Within* poured through me. Over the months and years, other songs would be sparked while I was reading, on retreat, or walking outside. During a solo pilgrimage around the coastal path of the Isle of Anglesey in Wales, *Be at Peace* was born.

Instrumentalists, including harpists, flutists, and guitarists, also bring melodies that are heard by those who are near death. From Canada, Kim has played flute for much of her life. She shares the story of her soulmate who loved her magic flute best of all:

A few weeks after receiving the news of his cancer diagnosis, my beloved was no longer able to go out. Sensing his sadness over missing my upcoming flute performance, I arrived at our next choir practice with my video camera in hand, and a rented high-end flute to ensure perfection.

The following morning, I opened his laptop and showed him the video recording of our performance of Don Besig's *Flying Free*. Later, my heart would sing every time I'd hear him ask his friends, nurses, care workers, and certain family members to open his laptop and watch the video of that song. Above and beyond the peace and joy the music offered to his soul, it also provided him with a way to connect and share with those he loved and appreciated, especially during times when conversation became difficult. And when speech stopped altogether, and his eyes failed to open again, I made sure that his gift of song remained the first thing he heard in the morning, and became his consistent lullaby at night.

Shortly after 11:00 a.m. on that fateful morning, I heard a calm but urgent voice beckoning me to the living room. The nurse pointed to his laptop and suggested I turn on the video he loved so much. "It will help him transition," she encouraged.

Fearing that I would not be able to boot up his computer fast enough, my attention went to my already assembled instrument. I wondered how I would ever be able to play under such extreme conditions, but I soon heard notes coming out of my flute. Surprisingly beautiful notes. Notes floating, vibrating, and resonating like I had never experienced before. They were the notes of a cherished song, *Hope*, written and gifted to me by my dear Maritime musician friend, the late John Ferguson.

At the song's completion, I held the final note as long as I could, letting it drift off into nothingness. I had completely run out of breath—and he had, too. There was a peaceful silence, seemingly accompanied by a subtle glow and inaudible buzzing in the room. His friend told me, "He took his final breath as you played your final note." The nurse exclaimed, "He rode your notes to Heaven."

Whether instrumental or vocal, classical or country, music has the power to speak to us and lead us outside ourselves.

Singing is a natural impulse

We each have a voice to produce beautiful harmonies. Without the need for instruments or technology, we, alone, may offer consoling—even ethereal sounding—melodies. For many, singing is a natural impulse throughout life and at a bedside.

It was natural for me to sing as I sat with my aunt. I had not yet heard of bedside singing, but I had sung with a variety of choirs since my high school days. On the evening of what would be her last, Aunt Lee was restless and uncommunicative. I spoke to her. I picked up her tome of a Bible and read to her. Unplanned, I began singing songs both from her religious tradition and others.

Singing was also a natural impulse for Kymn as she stood at her dad's side in the hospital. Perhaps like Kymn, you will hear a song that you must voice in that mystical moment:

My father died from complications of critical errors made by a surgeon. In the ICU, fighting for his life and on every kind of life support that there was, he hung on for six days. That gave everyone time to come to Florida where he was and say goodbye— but I don't think we knew at the time it was to say goodbye, but to come and honor him in his coma. People would come and go. My brothers and my mother would come and go because everyone had their lives to lead. And I, along with my stepmother and a dear friend of mine were there a lot. The friend was a very strong Quaker woman, like a rock in the midst of this very tumultuous situation.

On the morning of the day he ended up dying, my friend said to me, "He's ready." I was his health care proxy, and I had determined in talking with the doctor that my father had met all the criteria that he had set in his living will. Compassionate care had run its course, so we knew that as soon as we withdrew any of the life support, his death would be within one minute, actually. And so we gathered at his bedside. I gave the nurse a nod and we literally watched his heartbeat go from whatever it was down to zero.

And totally unexpectedly, totally unplanned, totally divinely ordered, I started singing this song: *All I ask of you is forever to remember me as loving you.* And certainly with tears rolling down my cheeks I was struggling to get the words out. But I nevertheless sang, and just had this deep sense of peace that my father knew how deeply he was loved. And that it wasn't just me singing to him; it was him also singing to me. [She sings the refrain and her tears come once again.] I sing this song and in a nanosecond return to his bedside.

Whether you sing or play an instrument, or cannot carry a tune, music is all around us. It's as though *music plays us*. As Steven from Massachusetts remarked, "When I hear a song, it puts me right back to where I was and what I was doing when I heard it." Just like Kymn and Jill who return to their dads' sides.

Inviting singers to a bedside

Bedside singers or Threshold singers continue an ancient tradition of gathering around the bed of the one dying. Whether the individual is recently diagnosed or actively dying, singers bring music which speaks to that person at that moment. Newly diagnosed, one young man advised, "Hey! I'm still alive. Give me Elvis!" One day may be good, another day not so much. Song selection changes and reflects the patient's needs on that day.

Singers are usually welcomed. When I visited a nursing and rehabilitation facility and explained that our newly formed Threshold Choir could offer bedside singing for the residents, the executive director had no hesitation. "Absolutely. That would be great. My mother lived in Vermont and when she was ill, and then dying, there were singers who visited her regularly. She so enjoyed the visits and the music, and looked forward to it. What a feeling of calm and peace and happiness. Of course you may come and sing here. Our residents will benefit."

Music brings people back to their whole life, their whole self. Whether or not they know the words, the beat encourages toe tapping, hand clapping, head bouncing, and smiles. It's as though they are drawn into the life force of the music and of the music maker:

> Today we find Elaine in bed. She is smiling and showing off her bright pink nail polish. I am moved to sing songs she would know from her time period. She joins in as she is able. We are laughing together—and she is dying. We intersperse our songs that have a quicker tempo, like *The Healing Water* (*I let the river carry me home*) with pensive ones like *A Place for You* (*where everything is new*). We end our time with *Be at Peace*, using it as a benediction.
>
> As the weeks pass, Elaine becomes subdued and occasionally admits to discomfort. She recognizes us but is not as engaged. We sing *Easy, rest easy.* We sing *You are loved, deeply loved. Thank you for all you have done / now it's your time to rest.* We know her religious affiliation, so we sing *Dona Nobis Pacem*.
>
> After her death, we visit the same facility to sing for others, and we pass by her room. I am moved to enter. I cross the now-empty space to the window, look out and notice patches of blue breaking through the cloudy sky, which reminds me of a Threshold song. I begin. *We are lifting you to the bright blue sky.* I choke and my singing partner finishes the verse. She and I have sung to Elaine for most of a year. This one was a harder dying for me.

Silence has its own sound

Do you remember *Sounds of Silence* by Simon and Garfunkel? Have you pondered the title? Really? Silence has a sound? Yes, silence does, which is why we sit in silence after each song, and do not immediately begin another. During that silence, the listener has space to hear the melody, a word or phrase, or wander into memories or associations stirred by the music. If we march from song to song, the vibrations of the first collide with the second, thereby intruding on and diminishing both.

Sit in silence—with or without song. Your sweet presence will be felt and appreciated. When we do not know what to say to this person at our side who is dying and leaving us, silence—like music—speaks for us. Silence stirs the deeper places within us. Be not afraid to visit because you are uncertain about proprieties. The silence that stretches across the distance uniting one heart with another is profoundly healing. In silent sitting, you speak volumes of your willingness to share, without judgment, the good, the bad and the ugly of someone else's journey. Both of you are the richer for it.

Whose songs?

We each listen to music that speaks to us. Persons who are living that long stretch from diagnosis to death don't want to hear dying music. I've had requests for show tunes, 40s music, and folk. Dan requested *A Dog named Shep* (actually titled *Old Shep*), written in 1933 and a favorite from his boyhood. We did not know it—the difficulty with taking requests. Instead, we enjoyed listening to his own singing along with the YouTube version.

On occasion, we encounter residents who want to sing to us. That's fine, too. I had been visiting Audrey but had never seen her; she was always hidden under the covers. On this day, her bed was empty and I went looking for her. I admitted to a nurse that I did not know what Audrey looked like. The nurse pointed to a woman who was finishing a sandwich in the hallway. That was Audrey. An aide arrived, returned Audrey to her room and settled her in bed. I knocked, entered, and told her who I was. I sang a few songs. She told me a sad story about an old boyfriend and sang a song that reminded her of him. Having warmed up, she continued with a song learned in childhood that she always sang at New Year's. On this visit, we enjoyed our one and only conversation. At another facility, a resident launched into *How Much is that Doggy in the Window?* You just never know.

There are songs from my parents' generation that everyone seems to know and that we may sprinkle into our Threshold repertoire. These include *You are my Sunshine*, *Over the Rainbow*, and *Amazing Grace*. For Navy veterans, I refreshed my recollection of *Anchors Aweigh*, learned long ago because my Dad and my Uncle Bill were Navy men. You may try *Blue Skies*, *What a Wonderful World*, *This Land is Your Land*, or whatever folk or pop songs are generationally appropriate.

Not everyone wants singing. I get it. Folks may be uncertain about the music or about the singer. But when a family or staff member hears us, they often approach patients, and suggest they try us and see. It is not unusual for our audition to become a regular gig for as long as we are needed.

We, too, try it out with someone new to determine whether it feels like a good fit. It is not always a good fit. We were asked to sing for a 96-year-old woman who was very hard of hearing. On our last visit she asked multiple times who we were. When we answered, she told us she couldn't hear us. Bending over her bed, perhaps a foot from her ear, we again identified ourselves—with no better results. As we were leaving she called out, asking where we were going. We answered and again were met with, "I can't hear you." It may be that under different circumstances with different visitors there would be a different reaction. It may be that music familiar to her would be heard. We certainly do not wish to cause any upset. In this case, we ceased our visits.

Then, again, song isn't always needed. Mr. Li was a professional musician—in fact, an orchestral conductor. He was residing at a skilled nursing facility and nearing the last measure of his life's score. We were asked to sing. I drove alone to the facility to see him and assess his condition.

I approached his room and stood in the doorway—that liminal space that is in-between, when you are no longer in the hallway but not yet in the room. I felt a peaceful, gentle wall that kept me out. It felt correct that I ought not to disturb the energy of his space; I remained in the doorway.

The room was dimmed. There was sufficient light to distinguish the features within but the window coverings were down and the lights were off. Instrumental classical music filled the air (although too loudly for my taste). Mr. Li lay perfectly still under the covers of his level bed. Why would

I—or anyone—wish to disturb this sanctuary? And so I did not. We did not have another opportunity to visit; he took his bow and exited this earthly stage two days later.

Threshold music

Bedside singers choose songs which speak to the spirit. Most of the music is written by other Threshold singers. This comforting and consoling yet unfamiliar *a cappella* music helps the listener separate and move on. Taize-like in their repetitive simplicity, the melodies are enhanced by harmony that flows *"from my heart to yours"* and noticeably change the vibration and atmosphere of a room. Indeed, I am privileged to have witnessed such a dramatic testament to the power of our Threshold music when three of us sang at a facility in Connecticut.

A recreation director called me, asking if we would sing to a group of patients rather than to the woman whom we had been visiting weekly for three or four months. The caller explained that our patient did not feel up for a visit, and since we had planned to come, well, would we consider singing to a group of patients? Given the time factor and the logistics of conferring with two other singers, I agreed on behalf of all of us.

We took the elevator to the second floor and entered the locked hallway. I could see into the room used for patient sing-alongs. One wall was lined with armchairs. An outside wall held several large, elevated beds—think pumpkin seats on wheels for mobility but large enough for a reclining adult. Additional seats in the middle of the room were occupied by persons with walkers or canes as well as by a man whose wife sat next to him in her wheelchair. We would not need the piano and organ at the front of the room.

As the three of us entered and put down our chairs, the director introduced us as "members of a Threshold Choir that will sing Christian songs." I quietly replied no, we would not sing Christian songs. After a moment I rose and offered my introduction. I explained that our nondenominational songs would be unfamiliar to them, but that they are soothing and comforting. I invited our listeners—residents and staff alike—to sit back, relax, and allow the melodies to wash over them. I gave them permission to close their eyes. I specifically admonished them not to applaud; we do not perform and do not expect any such acknowledgement. Our singing was our gift to them.

I do not recall every song we sang or in what order. Likely, we opened with *In the quiet of this moment / I am at peace / all is well.* Certainly we sang, *You are loved / deeply loved. Metta Sutta—May you dwell in the heart / May you be free from suffering*—was another. As is my practice, I permit Spirit to lead where we would travel. I could not have predicted our destination.

An absolutely amazing scene unfolded as we sang. The feeling tone of the room changed; that is typical. But what followed was remarkable. As I gazed out at the assembled circle, I observed this person slowly taking the hand of the next person. This one moving closer to the next one. That one putting an arm around a neighbor. Another offering a hug. Closed eyes, and soft, peaceful expressions. By the time we ended with my song—*May you be at peace / know that you are loved / May you be at peace / you're remembered*—there was a hush, a palpable peace in the room. More than that, the pairs had become trios, who themselves had reached out—until every person was in some way physically touching another.

We sat, breathing in the silence, before rising to leave. At the door, the director looked at me with a bewildered countenance. With a facial expression and tone of voice that broadcast wonder and amazement, she quietly and very slowly said, "I have never heard music like that before." I'm quite sure she'd never *felt* music like that, either.

Back in Massachusetts, my regular singing partner and I visited a new patient. Again relying on our Threshold repertoire, we could see George visibly relax, sink into his bedding and slowly close his eyes. When it was time to leave, he asked us to wait. After a bit he softly told us, "I could feel the love. Thank you, thank you. I hope you will come back and keep coming back."

As bedside singers, this is our intention for every person: to be in the vibration of love—and to keep coming back until death separates us.

CHAPTER 10

After They're Gone: How We Mourn and Remember

We are all just walking each other home.
—Ram Dass, American spiritual teacher,
psychologist, and author

The moment has come. Russell leans forward and opens his eyes. He had been lying very still and now this sudden movement. He exhales two short breaths. His children watch and wait for the inhale. Waiting for the inhale. Nothing's coming. Nothing's coming.

The last breath floats up on the wings of silence. The person before you is no more—at least, not in the ways you have seen and loved. The atmosphere has changed. The body—the vessel which Scripture calls a temple—feels hollow, empty, discarded by the one who no longer is in need of it.

It is obvious that the life force has gone. This body, which had kept itself at a constant temperature in life, is cooling in death. Touch the skin and it feels un-alive. But touch the skin closer to its heart center and it may yet be warm.

Treating the body as a temple

What if we treated this body as a temple? What if we offered gratitude for its creation, sustaining power, and amazing biological construction? How might we say goodbye to honor the dead and the container that protected mind, body, and spirit?

Some of us remain with the body. Others, who are not experienced with dying, do not realize that they can stay—or they are uncomfortable staying—and so leave soon after that last breath. Looking back, they may regret their earlier decision and choose differently when they find themselves at another bedside. This is what Jamie had to say about leaving the bedside of Douglas, who was her brother's life partner, and how she acted differently when her mother died years later:

> In the hospital room, we had surrounded Douglas' bed—with the priest at the foot, my brother and me up near his face, and on the other side were Douglas' mother and father. All of a sudden Douglas' identical twin brother threw himself on him, hugged him, and said, "You can go. It's OK." At that moment, Douglas started to stop breathing. It was as though he heard him. And he really just began to stop breathing. It took

about two or three minutes. We all were hushed and in awe. And then he left. It was really that experience where you could feel him and see him almost lift out of his body. It was very clear that his body was left there, dead, and that he was not there.

We stayed with Douglas' body for only a short while. We left and didn't come back. At some point the hospital people came and did what they do.

I didn't feel comfortable that we didn't stay with him. You know the body is going through a lot. It's not like you die, *bam*, and that's the end of that. It takes the body a while until it becomes completely cold and stiff. We can honor that body and the person who has just left it. It's such a sacred time and space. I just wish we had known to stay.

When her mom died, Jamie was ready, adapting rituals used by a friend and her sister when their mother had died. She recounts a very different experience this time around:

We chose to stay with my mother. It was like one, two, three o'clock in the morning—and it's such a special energy.

My sister is older than me but she was just following me. We had four or five women there. We lit candles, got warm soapy water, and I did some Hebrew prayers and chants. We washed her body and sort of anointed her with oils. And it was the women, you know, that did this. It was one of the most beautiful things in the world. We took our time.

My dad was in the room but he was just watching the women doing this thing.

It was so amazing. We picked out some cute clothes and dressed her for the flight from Florida back to Milwaukee. But we also picked out fancier clothes for after, to get her ready for burial.

The authorities came to pronounce her dead but we asked if we could leave her until the morning, because my brother was coming from Sacramento and hadn't yet arrived. They were very nice and agreed. So she got to stay the night and she was there when my brother came home and walked in the door.

When Manny died, all his children were present. His daughter explains the rituals they followed. As this and other stories show, each death and its aftermath takes its own special course:

It was the middle of the day when my father died, so there weren't the same energies. Still, it was amazing with my brother there and his special connection with our father. But there is one more thing.

After we did the whole ritual with my dad— washing and anointing him and chanting—and he was still kind of warm, and not gone in that regard, I had to lay down with him and snuggle with him and put my head on his chest. I was moved to do that. I swear to God it was like he was there—and I think he was there—and we had our last time together. I wrote about it in my journal and in a poem. It was harder for me. Maybe my dad didn't leave the Earth plane so soon, because it was harder for me to get that my dad had died; there was so much presence in a sense.

What you choose to do is right for you. Sit in silence, pray or offer a blessing with the body. One family went out for a meal:

So we left Dad there and went out to dinner. He was on the sofa with a blanket, like he was when he passed. When we returned, we walked in, poked our head in the door and saw him. The only difference was, he wasn't breathing. To honor him, we gave him one more night in his home. This was our way of blessing.

A daughter chose to sit with her mother's body. She describes how "magical and moving" it was:

I held the space energetically. Dad went back outside. They were living in a retirement home, so the nurses would be there quickly—but I didn't feel the need to call them and rush out right away. I didn't feel that would honor mom, by rushing out. I just honored that moment and that space. I cried,

even though I know there is so much more, but she
is my mom. For about an hour, I held the space for
her and for Dad and for the whole family.

We hold space in silence. I do the same at bedside, whether
for the living, the dying, or the dead. Silence, with its own
precious sound, is indeed magical and moving.

When considering what rituals you might adopt, reflect
how you get ready to lay children to rest for the night. You
provide a warm wash and clean clothes. You may offer a story,
lullaby, or evening prayer. As you gently and lovingly lay them
down, you straighten and pull up the covers so the body is
comfortable and cozy. You kiss them, perhaps stroke their hair
or offer a reassuring touch. You may bless them. You stand and
watch, marveling at the profound mystery that has created and
brought this embodied soul to you. You may put on a night
light. After another quiet moment, you turn, step outside the
room, and silently close the door. As you move away, you trust
and fully expect to see the child again.

You may do the same now for the empty body as you put
your loved one to rest:

- **Sit vigil. Be present.** For those who believe the spirit
  has left its earthly body, this time offers spiritual
  comfort during the journey away from the physical
  world. Some traditions encourage sitting vigil up
  to three hours after death for the separation to be
  complete. Stay for however long feels right for you.

- **Prayers and blessing.** Use prayers from your tradition, from Scripture texts or books of poetry and writings which were favorites. Speak out loud and let the gentle vibrations soothe the one who yet hears during this time of transition. Remember to maintain some sacred silence. Bless with water, oils, or laying on of hands.

- **Memories and stories.** We may fill this time with meaningful memories and stories of our times spent with the deceased. How reassuring for the departed to hear words of appreciation, admiration, and thanksgiving, to know we are loved and remembered as we travel beyond this earthly place.

- **Candles, scents, and music.** Use candles, scented or not, incense, dim or bright lights as you feel so moved to do, with or without music special to the one departing.

- **Bathing and dressing.**

  o By family or friends
     Not all of us are prepared to participate in the bathing, even if we remain present as loving witnesses. Of those who do lend a hand, the sacred nature is always preserved, whether or not the bathing is carried out by a group of similar gender—like Jamie and her women friends. *It's My Right: The Handmade Death of Herta Sturmann* follows the story of Herta, and the

death she chose by voluntarily stopping eating and drinking; her sons were with her, caring for her until and after death, building a personalized coffin and then laying her to rest. We always treat a body with the utmost care, dignity and respect.

o   By others
If we are not able to be involved directly but wish to honor the body and the one who inhabited it, then we may find someone else who can perform this ritual. Now more than ten years ago, I recall seeing the Japanese movie *Departures*. It recounts the professional training of a young man who learns and carries out the rituals used in preparing the dead for their final rest—for their departures.

Emerging from the current Green Burial trend, there is a nascent but growing number of individuals willing to come, bathe, and dress a body. If you wish, investigate whether a group is located near you.

Judaism has institutionalized the practice, establishing a *Hevra Kadisha* (holy society) that performs *Tahara* (purification), preparing a body for burial. Each Hevra has a separate group for women and for men. The tradition is rooted in the obligation for the living to give care for and respect the deceased.

Saying goodbye, turning away

Whether you remain with the body for a shorter or longer period, a time comes when you must say goodbye, turn away, and leave. How to say goodbye is an individual expression rising from a deep well within.

Perhaps you will throw yourself on the person, maybe lie down with the person. Perhaps you will let out an unexpected wail—as I did when I went to the funeral home to identify my husband's body and saw him for the last time.

Our public responses are conditioned by our culture, traditions, and personality. Perhaps it will be a subdued kiss or touch, or silent tears choked by grief, or constrained by our discomfort with showing emotion, even at a loved one's death. For others, vocal expressions of grief are typical.

Then again, you may come together at home and follow any number of private rituals. Some hand out slips of paper on which family members or guests write what they wished they had been able to say if they had had the opportunity. Then, one by one, the notes are tossed into a fire as the messages, like prayers, rise up to be heard by non-physical ears. Some may throw a party, a wake, or a viewing—with the recently deceased, smartly dressed for the occasion, in attendance. In addition to family and friends, some invite a wider community to pay their respects and reminisce, sending off the dearly departed on a high note of raucous song, laughter, and tears. Whether it's a quiet or flamboyant send-off, the reality of the meaning of the goodbye soon sinks in, and the work of grief begins.

Grieving your loss

Find someone to stay with you. If you are the friend, this is another way to offer valuable support. Your friend can be your anchor in the storm, a reassuring arm around your shoulders and a companion so you need not be alone—someone at your side as you struggle with feeling scared, overwhelmed, and even angry. You can feel safe, drawing comfort and knowing that a wider community supports you, now, and as you move forward.

Friends may assist with all the practical tasks that need attention. They can be your secretary, answering phones and taking messages; your cook to keep up your strength; and your personal assistant to help handle the arrangements of arriving family and guests, and funeral and burial services. If the person died at home, a helper may also arrange to return, dispose of, or store no-longer-needed medical goods, such as oxygen tanks, hospital beds, wheelchairs, medications, and supplies. Much is involved in putting a life to rest.

After the funeral or memorial

Staying in touch remains the most important gift during this time of bereavement. What this looks like will differ depending upon your relationship, but grieving individuals appreciate relief from isolation and solitary endeavors. How was your relationship before? What activities might you renew? Might you create opportunities for quiet moments together—such as nature walks, a glass of wine, or more active outings with others? Your invitations may not always be accepted, but it's a good idea to continue reaching out.

Whoever you are, remember that grieving a loss and adjusting to its related changes is a slow, hard process. Each of us processes loss in our own way, at our own pace. What is right for you is correct. Although there is no specified time period by which you will be done with grieving, be mindful and consider taking advantage of bereavement services through hospice, a counseling service, or your faith congregation. As a friend, stay in touch until most days are again sunny and bright.

PART FOUR

PREPARING TO SERVE

CHAPTER 11

So, Are You Ready to Begin?

The inward journey is about finding your own fullness.
—*Deepak Chopra, physician and author*

When a chorus is in harmony, each voice produces a melodic quality of tone at a particular pitch, which not only reproduces the written score but also offers a pleasing sound to the ear. And when other voices join in harmony, they add a different complementary line that works exquisitely with the melody line, creating a depth and expansion, a richness of juicy sound. Are you ready to play your part?

Sorting it out for yourself can be tricky. I've assembled a series of steps to help in that regard. In the end, you'll have gained greater self-awareness and an understanding of how to move forward.

Where you are now: admitting doubts and uncertainties

Take a breath and take heart if you have doubts and uncertainties. Perhaps you have never visited someone who was seriously ill or dying. Perhaps this was a visit you studiously avoided. Perhaps you now live with regret about an earlier choice you made—one that cannot be undone. You can make a different choice next time.

***

Exercise

Quiet yourself and take several deep breaths. Close your eyes if you wish. Ask yourself: Am I more comfortable with death and funerals than with visiting someone who is seriously ill and may be dying? Why? How do I feel I would behave around someone who is dying? Why? Record the answers you receive.

Looking inward allows you to be present to the fullness of you—from your anxieties to your successes. Paying attention to the voices in your head permits you to pause the tape in your mind, or to erase the unhelpful messages that undermine your confidence. Indeed, just imagining being with someone who is dying may have pushed that tape into fast-forward mode as it screams out reasons and justifications why you could never do that!

So here's my short list of possible excuses, and my brief responses. Please consider them.

- *I can't do that.* How do you know until you try?

- *I'm too busy.* Isn't it remarkable how, when something comes along that you wish to experience, you can always find the time?

- *I wouldn't know the person... well enough.* Do you know anyone well enough? Even your partner? Besides, you can discover each other together.

- *I wouldn't know what to do, what to say, or how to act.* This book has offered both general and specific guidance.

- *I don't want to catch what they have.* Facilities don't want you to catch anything either, which is why quarantines are in place. Fortunately, most illnesses are not contagious.

- *I'm too young, or too old, or too [fill in the blank].* Too young? Even kindergartners participate in intergenerational visiting programs. As a seventh-grader, my Scout troop spent a day with children with cerebral palsy. Too old? Some oldsters in assisted living reach out to less ambulatory residents. I can't help you with the blank.

- *I don't want to think about it.* What is *it*? Illness? Disease? Dying? Death? I suggest you think about death and dying, for it is a match that death wins—no exceptions, even for you. What's up for contention is how you go. Being with others facing their time may offer you a gentle entrance to consider your own good death.

- *I don't want to do it alone.* Ask a friend, a neighbor, or a congregational member.

- *It would be too emotional.* Maybe, maybe not. You might laugh through any tears and discover that dying people can be quite normal and interested in life.

- *They'll expect me to keep visiting forever.* Be clear about your schedule and commitment. And they may be thankful for the few times you do visit. Besides, it won't be forever; remember, they are dying.

- *I am allergic to places like nursing homes, rehabilitation facilities, or hospitals.* I can't help you here; there is no inoculation. However, each facility is different. You may be imagining a scene you will not find.

- *Let the staff do it; they're paid.* Yes, they are, albeit likely underpaid. Apart from that, the salient point is that there is inadequate staffing to provide personal and compassionate attention and conversation to each and every resident.

- *Let the family do it; it's their responsibility.* Caregiving is stressful under the best of conditions with the best of intentions. Moreover, when family members are dispersed; infirm; lack the requisite training, strength, and equipment for specialized care; or have insufficient financial resources when full-time caregiving demands that they cease employment; then additional assistance is reasonable and necessary.

Exercise

Take a pause and take several deep breaths. I hope you're feeling less anxious after reviewing this list. On a scale of 1 to 10—where 1 is turning away and 10 is turning toward someone who is dying—where are you at this moment?

You need not commit now, except to commit to further exploration of your inner life in all its fullness. For now, acknowledge the new understandings you hold. For now, take to heart this message: In whatever way you choose to move forward, you already have within you all that you need. You need only yourself and the willingness to take your first step forward.

Taking your first step

It may be that taking a step toward someone's bedside is your first time meeting or being with someone who is dying. If this seems like a significant barrier for you, then recognize that you have experienced first encounters in other moments of your life.

Exercise

Take a few moments to sit in silence and take several deep breaths.

Think back to a time when you were in a situation that was a "first time." It matters not what type of first it was. When you have one—you may recall more than one, but one is sufficient— write it down. Allow the memories to unfold. Write everything you remember. Pay particular attention to how you felt. How did you feel when you learned this first would occur? Were you nervous, afraid, cautious, and ready to run the other way? Were you excited, expectant, full of adventure, and impatient to get going? What mix of these feelings and others were sharing the space within you?

Take a few minutes to complete this inner work. It will serve as a foundation for what is to come. When you feel complete, return here and continue.

When you think about visiting someone for the first time, someone whom you do not know or have not seen recently, then you may be experiencing some of the same feelings as the ones you described in the exercise. On the other hand, if there has been a substantial period of time separating then and now, you may have accumulated tools—including reading this guide—that help you face new situations. Good for you!

Your cautious attitude comes from your fight-or-flight response. This response, coded in human DNA, was essential to our safety and well-being. It put us on hyper-alert for potential predator animals and dangerous conditions. Still today this response functions in similar ways when we encounter or imagine new situations.

Not every situation is as you believe it is. A student once asked me whether I was afraid to travel to a certain location. I instinctively knitted my brow in a reaction of surprise at the question because it had never occurred to me to be afraid. Why would I be afraid? I asked. Well, because A, B, or C might happen. Ah, the emphasis is on the *might* in that sentence, I explained. I don't look for, let alone expect, trouble.

At the bedside, what kind of trouble might there be? Take a good look at your feelings. If you are apprehensive, consider that it may be your nerves—that is, your adrenaline sparking from your own fight-or-flight response. Calm yourself. Take a few deep breaths. Tell yourself—out loud: All is well. Smile. Take another deep breath and take your second step forward.

Taking your second step

We need to identify your *why*. We've addressed typical doubts and uncertainties. We've recalled how you have successfully handled firsts in your life. Now we look to identify your foundational principle in moving forward. What is your intention? What is your motivation? Why will you take the time and make the effort to be with someone who is dying?

Exercise

Prepare for serious, honest reflection. The most important question may be this one: your why. A program or the person(s) you visit will come to rely on you and look forward to your presence. Is your why strong enough to sustain you through the long term? Dying can be a waiting game. How will you integrate visits with personal, family, work, and social pulls on your time? You need not have all the answers now. Indeed, perhaps not all these questions are relevant to your life's circumstances. Nonetheless, I suggest it is reasonable to have raised these questions for you to consider now or at a later time.

Back to the overarching question: Why will you serve others in this way? What is your intention, hope, and desire in visiting? Quiet. Breathe. Receive. Record.

It will be valuable to refer to your responses and remind yourself of a larger purpose to which your actions contribute.

Permit me to share why I walk with others on their end-of-life journeys. A camp song speaks about greeting someone with a joyful and open heart. I want to bring and be joy and peace to the one in the bed and to family members. I want them to feel the joy of this life—even at its end—and anticipate the *joy on the other side*, as Ruthie Foster sings. And I want them to see, as I do, that when breath ceases, the sacred silence will stand as witness to the awesome mystery of their life—and of life itself.

Sometimes, I say I found myself here, or I was drawn to this—or my path (or Spirit) led me here. Other times, I pause and notice the signs and the moments; yet, with astonishment and with wonder, I shake my head and exclaim, "How *did* I get to where I am now?" Martin Luther declared, "Here I stand." Like him, I say, "here I stand," sharing what I have learned thus far to encourage you to visit at bedside and share another's final journey.

Can you begin to trace the thread back through the warp and weft of your life's tapestry that has brought you to this moment?

Taking your third step

Being with someone and their family who are facing a challenging diagnosis and an emotionally charged present and future is hard. Their fears trigger yours. Their anxieties spark yours. Another's decline toward death puts you face to face with your own, for one day you, too, will lie in the bed. The specter of death raises those big existential questions: *What is the meaning of life? Of my life? What is my place in all of this? What is death? What happens to me after death?* I encourage you to take some moments and consider your beliefs. Having no belief is in and of itself a belief.

Exercise

Take a few deep breaths, quiet yourself, close your eyes if you wish, and ask yourself these questions. What is life? What is death? Do we die? What does that mean? Do you die? What does that mean? Does life continue after death?

If the language I am using does not resonate with you, then substitute language of your own to express what you believe today about life and the end of physical life. I say "what you believe today" because unless you are inflexible and close-minded, experiences and people you encounter may completely alter or nuance your current understanding. (Recall the brother who now absolutely knows his deceased dad came to him but doesn't yet know what to do with that.)

Yes, these are big questions. Feel free to swim in the shallows or to dive deep—as you are so moved. It's up to you. And yes, this may be the first time you have given any attention to a deeper contemplation of these questions. It's not unusual for many of us to avoid thinking about death at all costs.

Having awareness of your beliefs is vitally important. When we behave or speak out of habit rather than from a conscious, intentional present moment, we may bring with us that which is better left behind. For example, you may feel compelled to pray for an outcome other than death. You may see your visit as an opportunity to save, to begin a proselytizing conversation. Perhaps you tend to spout platitudes—"it is God's will"; "God will not give you more than you can bear"; "if God brings you to it, He will bring you through it"; and so forth. Do your research and you will discover that many dying persons consider these words empty, burdensome, offensive, and unwanted. Better to drop your personal beliefs along with the clichés at the door.

Having awareness of our beliefs and of our doubts and uncertainties brings us to an awareness of ourselves. The first person we need to sit with is our self—we need to face our own mortality. For all of us, one day we will make this journey. When we can sit comfortably with our self in an attitude of acceptance and even hope and joy, we can sit with others, allowing the dying to contemplate their lives even as we have contemplated ours.

Taking your fourth step

Inner work reminds us to clear out our mental chatter, the trivial thought loops that seem to have no pause or stop button. From your point of view about the type of care or treatment possibilities, to how a dying person *should* be, leave that all behind. Be alert to your "monkey mind," which jumps from whether you have time to run errands, make dinner, and pay bills to what's on your social calendar for tomorrow or the weekend. You are at the bedside to be with and to focus on the person before you. Direct your thoughts and your heart there.

I spend quiet time in preparation prior to a visit to refocus my attention and my energy to the person I am going to see. I intend that my personal issues will be put to the side. I intend that our meeting will be for the highest and best of all, for each of us. And I always intend that my heart is open and that holy love flows through me.

External indicators give others an immediate impression of you. How do you express who you are and what you are feeling? You have the opportunity to bring brightness, joy, and serenity to each person and to every moment.

Exercise

Who are you? This is not a competition. You have your own unique gifts, talents, and ways of being. I invite you to sit quietly, take those deep breaths, and scan your body, your emotions, and your thoughts. Then list your many and varied positive expressions, and bring them with you into the room of another.

Taking your fifth step

You've been at bedside before, so you know what to expect. Right? If you've seen one, you've seen them all. Right? *Wrong.* And if you have not been here before, what do you anticipate? For each of you, what is your vision of the sights, sounds, and smells of the experience?

Exercise

Take your deep breaths and settle into quiet. Ask yourself, "What do I expect when I visit someone?" Pause. Reflect. Write whatever surfaces for you, without censoring or second-guessing.

Each visit, even to the same person, is a first visit; it is different. Their emotional, mental, or physical condition changes, often in the same day. Dealing with dying can be an emotional roller coaster, with quick ups and downs.

For someone with dementia, this is especially true. Will the person remember you? Or will you be a stranger with an unknown agenda? Will the person be violent or agitated today? Try not to take any remarks or situations personally.

I recall one early visit when a patient looked at one of the visitors and commented unflatteringly about her body. In a huff, that person abruptly stood up, declared she would no longer visit that person, and left. On every other later occasion, we found that patient warm, pleasant and eager to have us return—which we did until she died.

We adopt a posture of being focused on this moment, being fully present. On this person. On this person's mood and words—or silence—as well as their physical condition and needs. We hold the space, practicing compassion without expectation or return. We open our hearts, our eyes, our ears, and our arms, and we accept them. With all they have lost and are losing, we allow them to be who they are, without apology or explanation. We honor who they are and the essence of their being. We give back to them the dignity they may feel slipping away.

Taking your sixth step

Death comes to us all, regardless of age. Car accidents, undiagnosed medical conditions, and childhood diseases may lead to a terminal prognosis. Pediatric palliative care programs focus on long-term comfort care for children and adolescents with chronic illnesses. Memory care programs support those with dementia.

While my experience has been with the elderly, you may find yourself drawn to journey with a different age group.

(Of course, your family or friends will attract your love and attention, regardless.) Having a preference is not unusual. Educators choose to work with students of a particular grade or age range. Medical workers routinely choose a specialty, as do attorneys. We seek to find a good, comfortable fit that works for everyone in the relationship.

Exercise

After your breaths, get quiet, and pause. Ask yourself what type of person or population group you feel drawn to at this time. Have you had experience or training with folks of a particular age or situation? Do you feel open and available to everyone, or to one group in particular? Record your reactions.

Taking your seventh step

Our inner work concludes with this last step. It's now up to you to take the next step. We have considered our doubts, beliefs, expectations, and preferences. We have learned much more about our inner landscape, especially relative to death and dying, and our willingness and capacity to journey with others to their final breath.

What else do you need to know? What else would increase your confidence to have the courage to knock on someone's door? What would help you feel ready for a bedside visit? As with the preceding exercises, there is no right or wrong answer.

Each exercise has enabled you to discover more of yourself, to increase your self-awareness. Knowing yourself, you know better how to be with another.

Exercise

Quiet yourself and take a few deep breaths. What do you need to feel more confident and competent at the bedside of someone who is dying? What do you need to feel ready? Do you have what you need?

You may need experience. Lacking it, you hesitate. I trust this book has given you much to help you feel prepared. But I cannot give you experience. For that, you must take a breath, knock on a door and enter. Nothing less will suffice.

Experience only comes from crossing someone's threshold. You may delay your visit, always wanting and feeling you need more. More information. More understanding. But it is only by visiting people who are dying—whether they are still ambulatory or already far along on the road to passing over—that you will acquire what you think you need. You must *go* there. When you show up and bring your authentic, caring self, your precious presence will be the memory that lasts—for you, for your new friend, for family members. You, being fully present and having the courage to care, are the essential ingredient at bedside. You are enough. And when you go, you will be in good company.

In good company

Our moving toward loss, toward the dying and toward the bedside puts us in good company on a path that has been well trod over thousands of years. We are encouraged by our spiritual communities and their sacred texts, as well as by our natural instincts toward empathy for others, whether stranger or friend. When my oldest daughter was about three years old, we were walking in a mall when she saw a family with a little girl. My daughter went up and hugged the girl. The parents were aghast that their daughter was approached in this way by a stranger, despite the innocent overture. From where does this kindness spring? It is always within each of us, although it can be either stunted or supported.

Serendipitously, in 1982, the same year this daughter was born, Anne Herbert was credited with writing the words "practice random acts of kindness and senseless acts of beauty" on a placemat in a Sausalito, California, restaurant. This became a kindness slogan, with bumper stickers and the creation of a Random Acts of Kindness Day (February 17) as well as a World Kindness Day (November 13). Ten years later in 1992, *USA Magazine* initiated Make a Difference Day, celebrated on the fourth Saturday in October. Both of these endeavors promote a similar vision: encouraging good deeds of kindness and making a difference, including helping or cheering up someone—for no reason other than to express connection, community, and compassion. Each year on these designated days, individuals and groups perform spontaneous acts of kindness in their communities. Surely, reaching out to be in touch with or visiting someone who is ill, lonely, or dying is an ideal act of kindness, which does make a difference—on any day.

Based on religious tenets, various spiritual communities have formalized our love of others and our offering of aid in times of need. As long as 7,500 years ago for what would later be called Hinduism, and 5,500 years ago for what is known today as Buddhism, visiting the sick was an important responsibility. Not only family members but also many from outside the family came to call. In addition to visiting, taking care of the elderly and sick was a family obligation. Later, the Buddha would observe that everyone's life experiences include birth, aging, illness, and death—each of these a natural part of the human life cycle. We would do well, therefore, to learn how to respond when it is our turn to face one or another of these conditions—or to help others.

Within Judaism, the tradition of visiting the sick is a *mitzvah* (a good deed) that dates back thousands of years. The Talmud explains, "Just as God visits the sick, so too is it incumbent upon us to imitate God and visit the sick." Jewish communities often organize a *Bikur Cholim* (Visiting the Sick) Society, whose members visit those who are ill, sharing good cheer, and reminding them of their continuing place in the congregation.

When Christianity was established, it is unsurprising that it would continue the traditions of Judaism, out of which Christianity grew. Jesus, a practicing Jew, celebrated connections with all sorts of people. He spoke to the Samaritan woman, and invited a tax collector to be an apostle. Believers yet today are exhorted to love their neighbors as themselves and to welcome the stranger. In the New Testament Letter of James we read of the duty to be "doers of the word and not hearers only" and to visit and "care for orphans and widows in their affliction."

The corporal and spiritual works of mercy, which are based on Jesus' teachings, have long been part of the Christian tradition. These works were offered as guides, showing believers how they might put Jesus' words into practice. For example, one spiritual work of mercy is to "comfort the sorrowful." The United States Conference of Catholic Bishops (USCCB) explains that showing "comfort" includes listening to and being present for those who are grieving, because "[a] few moments of your day may make a lifetime of difference to someone who is going through a difficult time." The corporal works of mercy include visiting the sick. The USCCB encourages visitation, saying, "Those who are sick are often forgotten or avoided. In spite of their illness, these individuals still have much to offer to those who take the time to visit and comfort them."

When Islam formed, the Prophet Mohammed continued the admonition to visit the sick. Visits are to be made whether or not the sick person is Muslim, and whether or not the sick person is known or a stranger. It is said that despite Mohammed's many and varied responsibilities in the community and at home, he always made time to visit those who were unwell. When we take the time to offer comfort and support, and to share in the sufferings of others, our presence shows our love and concern.

In the end, only kindness matters.
So sang Jewel, the singer-songwriter. There are many reasons for spending time with someone. You may have strong family or friendship ties. You may be moved to follow the example of 12-year-old Trevor McKinney, who launched a goodwill movement known as "Pay it Forward" in the book and film by the same name. Now aware of the multitudes that are hungry to hear your voice, you may bring music and song to brighten someone's day and lighten their spirit. Being there at bedside may be your way of making a difference, of making the world a better place—one kindness at a time, beginning in your hometown.

Despite constant change, one certainty is that each of us comes into this life and each of us goes out of this life. Others made careful, compassionate, and loving preparations celebrating the wonder of birth. May we now do the same to celebrate this wonder of death. On this sacred, mystical, and magical journey, may we have the courage to care—to be fully present with each one who is dying.

CONCLUSION

One person can make a difference.
Every person must try.
—*President John F. Kennedy*

I trust you now know much more about how to support someone—and their family—when you hear the words, "I'm dying."

You've learned how our physical dying process unfolds, and how our marvelous bodies know how to close down, often without pain or discomfort. You're ready for the emotional swings as we each react to the news of our approaching death. You're aware that we all die differently based on our personality and preferences. And that these differences are best honored, even celebrated. That's the *what*.

You've also been clued in to the *how*, including the ten guiding principles. You know to ask what people want or need. And to wait and ask again. When they feel you will not judge them or their replies, you'll be taken into their confidence.

You understand that death and dying are deeply personal experiences, and that each of us struggles with our own set of challenges. At their end—whether it's being outside under the starry sky, dying with the Hallelujah chorus blasting away, or just creating an intimate setting with candlelight and hand holding—you know how to honor them in the ways they choose.

You've been fortified with multiple lists of specific suggestions outlining what you can actually do to help. From diagnosis to death, valuable options exist for everyone. You'll know what fits for you, depending on your relationship to the one dying and on the degree of trust you've formed.

The *where* is for you to search in your wider community. Certainly, there are family, friends, and neighbors. I also hope you will consider serving in a hospice; or as a volunteer in a hospital, retirement center, assisted living community, or nursing home. People living entirely on their own may also welcome your caring presence. Indeed, should the Village Movement prove successful, there will be increasing numbers of elders living at home and needing volunteer help as they "age in place."

You've gained a depth and breadth of understanding of the meaning of being fully present with someone who is dying. And you've identified your particular qualities, skills, and talents, which you can uniquely express to give people the comfort they need.

Now you just need to...*go*. You have been well-prepared and you have what you need. Movement will lead you toward the place that is your perfect fit for this time of your life. Together, we can cherish and honor the end of life, as beautifully as we do life's beginning. Go ahead. Take your next step and show others your courage to care.

AFTERWORD

One morning as I was writing this book, I was thanking spirits who are supporting me on this journey and I heard myself also thanking the spirits of those who have died. I heard, "We wish to tell you something to share with others." I sat down at my computer, placed my fingers on the keyboard and waited. As I close this book, I leave you with these words from them, who through me, have reached out to you:

Don't leave us alone

Don't forget us

We are still here and alive in our own way

You may never know how much your open heart and your generous spirit is a precious gift to us and indeed to yourself

But then you are not walking with us to gain anything material or to have any expectation of reward

You are walking together with us because we are all on this journey together and for a time—however brief—you have been our companion on the road.

Thank you

Blessings upon you

Amen. Go in peace.

SOURCES AND NOTES

Chapter 1

1. Importance of physical touch to well-being: https://www. healthline.com/health/touch-starved; https://greatergood. berkeley.edu/article/item/why_physical_touch_matters_ for_your_well_being; and Denworth, Lydia. "The Social Power of Touch." *Scientific American Mind*, July/August 2015, pp. 30–39.

2. Numbers of aging population: https://www.pewresearch. org/fact-tank/2010/12/29/baby-boomers-retire/; and https://www.prb.org/aging-unitedstates-fact-sheet/.

3. The Basic Christian Community movement of the 1960s and 70s, which took on different expressions depending upon the country, encouraged the formation of small groups for study, prayer, and support. Today, congregational study and social groups offer opportunities for members to develop stronger ties with each other: https://www.

encyclopedia.com/religion/encyclopedias-almanacs-transcripts-and-maps/basic-christian-communities.

4. Caring for a spouse with dementia: https://www.caregiver.org/caregiver-statistics-demographics; and health risks of caretakers: www.caregiver.org/caregiver-health.

5. Number of persons 65+ and number anticipated having dementia: https://www.prb.org/aging-unitedstates-fact-sheet/.

6. Dr. Atul Gawande's initiative has been picked up by various health care providers. One NODA (No One Dies Alone) program in Massachusetts is at Baystate Medical Center: https://www.baystatehealth.org/news/2019/11/no-one-dies-alone-volunteer-interview.

7. Number of Americans who want to die at home: https://palliative.stanford.edu/home-hospice-home-care-of-the-dying-patient/where-do-americans-die/.

Chapter 2

1. Saul, Peter, M.D. "Let's talk about dying." TEDxNewy. November 2011. www.ted.com/talks/peter_saul_let_s_talk_about_dying?language=en#t-396528.

2. Sundowner symptoms of persons with more severe dementia include paranoia, violence, and wandering,

especially in the late afternoon and early evening as the sun goes down. https://sundownerfacts.com/symptoms/.

3. Sacrament of the Sick: https://www.usccb.org/prayer-and-worship/sacraments-and-sacramentals/anointing-of-the-sick.

4. Feast of the Assumption: https://nationaltoday.com/feast-assumption/.

5. *Memorare* Catholic prayer: http://www.scborromeo.org/prayers/memo.pdf.

Chapter 3

1. Kübler-Ross, Elisabeth, MD. *On Death and Dying: What the Dying Have to Teach Doctors, Nurses, Clergy and Their Own Families.* New York: Scribner, 1969. p. 75 and 133, about begging for what we need and about coping strategies.

2. "Be Glass" visualization, courtesy Windy Woodland, taught during her meditation classes, Indianapolis, Indiana, 1990s.

3. End-of-Life Doula or Death Doula assists in the dying process, much like a midwife or doula does with the birthing process. A doula assists the one dying and the family with end-of-life planning; legacy projects; scheduling; emotional and spiritual support; vigil sit-

ting; offering information; and more—helping them cope with death through recognizing it as a natural and important part of life. Professional certification is available for doulas. I hold a professional certificate.

4. "We may not need words...." from *Can I Stand Here for You?* by Kate Munger ©1/2011. https://www.youtube.com/watch?v=iDMFt9d5NaM sung by Melanie DeMore, words and music by Kate Munger (kateamunger@gmail.com).

5. Stanford Medicine Letter Project: https://med.stanford.edu/letter.html.

6. Lonegren, Sig. *Labyrinths: Ancient Myths and Modern Uses.* Glastonbury, U.K.: Gothic Image Publications, 1991. I took a class with Sig. See images of the labyrinth at Chartres, a cathedral in France: www.google.com/search?q=chartres+labyrinth&tbm=isch&chips=q:chartres+labyrinth.

Chapter 4

1. One source for cultural differences: https://www.cancer.net/coping-with-cancer/managing-emotions/grief-and-loss/understanding-grief-within-cultural-context.

2. INELDA (International End-of-Life Doula Association): www.inelda.org.

3. Federal non-discrimination statement for health care: https://www.hhs.gov/programs/topic-sites/lgbt/accesstohealthcare/

nondiscrimination/index.html. However, a new rule, which
was adopted by the Trump Administration and took effect
August 2020, changes and seems to eliminate protections
in health care for our LGBTQ members. See https://
www.npr.org/2020/06/12/876357667/new-government-
rule-removes-non-discrimination-protections-for-lgbtq-
in-health-care.

4. Health Care and the LGBTQ community: Zeitlin,
Dave. "Finding Life in Death." *The Pennsylvania Gazette*,
March/April 2020, pp. 32–39 https://thepenngazette.
com/finding-life-in-death/.

5. Everybody Counts! Here's how one school implemented
the disability awareness program: https://sainti.org/school/
about/news-events/everybody-counts-2019/.

6. Shapiro, Joseph. "One man's covid-19 death raises the worst
fears of many people with disabilities." *NPR*, 7/31/2020.
Texas case of 46-year-old family man, a Black man, a
man who was a paraplegic, who was hospitalized with
covid-19. His treatment was ended and he died. Also,
Roger Severino, Director of the Office for Civil Rights,
announced guidelines protecting the elderly and persons
with disabilities from receiving limited care.

7. smith, s.e. "How Disability Helps Me Find Life in Death."
Catapult Magazine, 3/21/18. https://catapult.co/stories/
how-disability-helps-me-find-life-in-death.

Chapter 5

1. The Covenant of the Rainbow: Genesis 9:11–17.

2. Levitation—and saints: https://www.historydisclosure.com/teresa-de-avila-levitating-saint/.

3. Fellowships of the Spirit. www.fellowshipsspirit.org.

4. Rinpoche, Songal. *The Tibetan Book of Living and Dying*. San Francisco: Harper One, 2002. p. 172–3 re rainbow bodies.

5. Dr. Sandra Bertman, noted thanatologist: http://www.sandrabertman.com/files/about.html.

6. Cayce and Moody are listed in the Recommended Reading.

7. Newton, Michael, PhD. *Journey of Souls: Case Studies of Life between Lives*. Woodbury, Minn.: Llewellyn Publications, 1994.

8. Newton, Michael, PhD. *Destiny of Souls: New Case Studies of Life between Lives*. Woodbury, Minn.: Llewellyn Publications, 2000.

9. Schucman, Helen. *A Course in Miracles: Based On The Original Handwritten Notes Of Helen Schucman—Complete & Annotated Edition*. Circle of Atonement, 2017.

10. Selig, Paul. *I am the Word*. Tarcher Perigee, 2010.

11. Hicks, Jerry and Hicks, Esther, et al. *The Astonishing Power of Emotions: Let Your Feelings Be Your Guide.* Book 4 of 7 of the Teachings of Abraham.

12. Roberts, Jane. *Seth Speaks: the Eternal Validity of the Soul.* Amber-Allen Publishing, 1994. One of 12 books.

13. Peggy Black and her team bring *Morning Messages*: https://morningmessages.com/.

14. For *Heavenletters*: http://heavenletters.org/god-speaks.html.

Chapter 6
1. Dr. Masaru Emoto: https://thewellnessenterprise.com/emoto/.
2. Denworth, Lydia. "The Social Power of Touch." *Scientific American Mind*, July/August 2015, pp. 30–39.

Chapter 7
1. Robin Williams played *Patch Adams* in the film by the same name, 1998. The real Patch Adams was a physician and clown. https://www.patchadams.org/.

2. Norman Cousins writes of his cancer recovery through laughter. https://sites.google.com/site/laughofflife/page-1. Cousins talks about positive emotions and health: https://media.laughteryogaamerica.com/pdf/ncousins-interview.pdf.

3. Free advanced planning guide, be prepared kit: https:// www.advancelifeplanning.org/.

4. Notes to My Family is another organizing tool for personal, medical, and financial information: https://hospicegiving. org/resources/#NTMF.

5. *Five Wishes*, available from Hospice or online for talking about and documenting your care and comfort wishes: www.Five-wishes-sample.pdf and https://fivewishes.org/ five-wishes/health-care-systems/five-wishes-for-hospice.

6. For suggestions to start conversations about health and care through the end of life, see https://theconversationproject.org/.

7. For talking about death, see: Hebb, Michael. "What happens when Death is what's for Dinner?" TED Talk, June 29, 2013. https://www.youtube.com/watch?v=4DT0aMfFtuw. Explore the Death Café, a scheduled non-profit get-together for the purpose of talking about death over food and drink. www.deathcafe.com.

8. *Ho'oponopono* is a Hawaiian practice of reconciliation and forgiveness. The Hawaiian word translates into English simply as *correction*.

9. Visit www.Storycorps.org to schedule an interview, view archives, and more.

Chapter 8

1. "We cannot follow you…" from *Keep Watch* by Becky Reardon © March 2005. http://www. beckyreardonmusic.com/.

2. Dornell, Marian Cannon. *Unicorn in Captivity.* Georgetown, Ky.: Finishing Line Press, 2015.

3. Kirtan Hindu chants, Gregorian or Taize singing, and Threshold Choir songs are different musical forms. Kirtan is devotion in the form of music: https://www.youtube. com/watch?v=Y2A7CYuuVg8. Tibetan Healing Sounds: https://www.youtube.com/watch?v=x6UITRjhijI. Gregorian chants: https://www.youtube.com/watch?v=eb_J46Eprqo. Hebrew Sh'ma Yisrael: https://www.youtube.com/ watch?v=djephsMyZHI. Threshold Choir International music: https://thresholdchoir.org/catalog/products.

4. Taize [repetitive] singing: "Stay with me, remain here with me, watch, and pray," https://www.youtube.com/ watch?v=FCr2tn4yYKY based on Matthew 26:38–41.

5. *I'd Love You to Want Me* by Lobo, 1972. Listen on YouTube.

6. *Deeply Loved* by Marilyn Power Scott ©2007 Gesundheit Publishing. www.gesundheitpublishing.com. Also titled *I Am Loved.* Listen at https://gesundheitpublishing.com/ spirit-of-harmony-songs/.

7. *Dear One* by Penelope Salinger ©2008. Email mn8joy@yahoo.com. Listen at https://www.youtube.com/watch?v=CiZJXxjwxjU&list=UUK5D-opYuA1iIlNdq0H-d6w&index=3.

8. *Passing Time* (*Your soul knows the way….*) by Terry Garthwaite ©2011. tgnjoysounds15@gmail.com.

9. *Be at Peace* by Linda Bryce ©2017. Sheet music available from the author.

10. *Tonglen* Buddhist meditation: https://www.youtube.com/watch?v=QwqlurCvXuM led and explained by Pema Chödrön, an American Buddhist widely known for her down-to-earth interpretation of Tibetan Buddhism for Western audiences.

11. *Beautiful Gate* (*We can't arrive early….*) by Kate Munger ©7/2009. Email kateamunger@gmail.com.

Chapter 9

1. *You are Beautiful* by Kate Schuyler ©2016. Email schuykate@gmail.com. Listen at https://www.youtube.com/watch?v=W-ZrHS9Towo.

2. The vibrations of music also change wine (and food). A Canadian winery accidentally discovered that the music they regularly played, especially drumming, produced better-tasting wine. The winery then installed a music studio inside its winery to ensure ongoing positive

influences as well as a venue for musicians. Reported on the Netflix show *Restaurants on the Edge*—"Frequency Winery," Okanagan Valley, Kelowna, BC, Canada—season 1, episode 7.

3. Healing power of music: https://www.prevention.com/life/a20463031/how-music-heals/.

4. Music as medicine. *The Impact of Healing Harmonies*, Harvard Medical School: https://hms.harvard.edu/sites/default/files/assets/Sites/Longwood_Seminars/Longwood%20Seminar%20Music%20Reading%20Pack.pdf, one of multiple sources.

5. Music for stroke patients: https://www.sciencefocus.com/news/music-therapy-for-stroke-patients-improves-brain-and-motor-function/.

6. Music for persons with Parkinson's and dementia, including Alzheimer's: https://www.youtube.com/watch?v=4abaiZZIqHU.

7. Music and Memory Foundation and research: https://musicandmemory.org/music-brain-resources/current-research/.

8. *Alive Inside*, 2014 film: www.Aliveinside.org.

9. *Rest Easy* by Marilyn Power Scott © 2009 Gesundheit Publishing. www.gesundheitpublishing.com. Listen at https://www.youtube.com/watch?v=weUMFm9CurI.

10. *Safe in the Arms of Love* by Patricia Hallam © 2015. Email pahallam@comcast.net. Listen at https://www.youtube.com/watch?v=LXWOAPNXfII.

11. *In the Quiet* by Irene Favreau ©2010. Email ifinca@aol.com.

12. *All I Ask of You* by Gregory Norbet, OSB. Listen at https://www.youtube.com/watch?v=Y9FFnNIovNo.

13. *The Healing Water* (*I Let the River*) by Penelope Salinger ©2012. Email mn8joy@yahoo.com. Listen at https://www.youtube.com/watch?v=j1Ecr9w-fRM at 2:11 (Note: It's usually not sung this quickly).

14. Both *A Place for You* (Listen at https://www.youtube.com/watch?v=kQUITRsAde4) and *Bright Blue Sky (We are lifting you to the bright blue sky...)* © Melanie DeMore. www.melaniedemore.com.

15. *From My Heart to Yours* by Maria Culberson ©2004. culbersonm@gmail.com.

16. *Old Shep* sung by Red Foley. Written in 1933 but first recorded in 1935. Listen at https://www.youtube.com/watch?v=yxSTKXnw7wc.

17. *Metta Sutta*, words from Buddhist text, music by unknown, arranged by Kate Munger. Email kateamunger@gmail.com. Listen to a different musical arrangement of *Metta Sutta* by Robert Gass at https://www.youtube.com/watch?v=3WXLnxABZpI, www.springhillmedia.com.

Chapter 10

1. Herta Sturmann's story *It's My Right: the Handmade Death* on vimeo.com/359407878.

2. *Departures* (2008). Available at https://www.youtube. com/watch?v=V97h623Zqqk.

3. Random Acts of Kindness at https://www.randomactsof-kindness.org/rak-week. Kindness ideas at https://kindness. org/?gclid=CjwKCAjwz6_8BRBkEiwA3p02VbMqIJ_ W6d9Nk9PQXFfVCKRPnzOThS4xdKP-L2H4XmB-174nMGZJg4RoCHqYQAvD_BwE. Servicespace is another source of ideas and connection at https://www. servicespace.org/about/?gclid=CjwKCAjwz6_8BRBkEi-wA3p02VRNsGWGy18ZAVOwzJD1KUmiCuFJ81AA-5fOG-8cj51TDhfy41Xv-hhBoCGDgQAvD_BwE. 100 Acts of Kindness for Kids at https://www.coffeecupsandcray-ons.com/100-acts-kindness-kids/. Make a Difference Day at https://nationaldaycalendar.com/national-make-a-differ-ence-day-fourth-saturday-in-october/.

4. The Talmud's instruction on visiting the sick: https:// www.aish.com/atr/Visiting_the_Sick.html.

5. Be doers of the word, and not hearers only: James 1:22–27.

6. United States Conference of Catholic Bishops: www.usccb. org. Spiritual works of mercy at https://www.usccb.org/ beliefs-and-teachings/how-we-teach/new-evangelization/

jubilee-of-mercy/the-spiritual-works-of-mercy. Corporal works of mercy at https://www.usccb.org/beliefs-and-teachings/how-we-teach/new-evangelization/jubilee-of-mercy/the-corporal-works-of-mercy.

7.   Visiting the sick in the Islamic tradition: https://sunnah.com/riyadussalihin/6.

8.   *Pay it Forward* (2000). The Philosophy of Pay it Forward at https://www.youtube.com/watch?v=URwXr144hlI.

Chapter 11

1.   Ruthie Foster. "Joy on the Other Side." *The Truth According to Ruthie Foster.* Blue Corn Music, 2009. Listen on YouTube at https://www.youtube.com/watch?reload=9&v=Vi-TDhGDoRk.

2.   The song I sing to prepare myself is *Holy Love* by Patricia McKernon Runkle ©1983. Email pmrunkle@gmail.com.

Conclusion

1.   The Village Movement to "age in place": https://www.aarp.org/home-family/friends-family/info-2017/age-in-place-village-movement-fd.html.

APPENDICES

The Talk You Must Have Now: End-Of-Life Documents

This isn't a conversation to have in an emergency room or an intensive care unit. It isn't easy and we don't want to face it; but now is the moment to make time to say, "This is what I want when I am dying."

My friend had mixed feelings about her dad's birthday. Happy that he was around for another year. Unhappy during that moment when he took her aside, handed her a sealed envelope and said, "This is my gift to you and my family. I am taking care of this now so when my time comes, you will have the information you need to make medical or surgical decisions guided by my preferences for comfort or desperate cure and, eventually, concluding my estate. Your grief will not be compounded by the disarray of my personal affairs. These are my will, financial accounts, medical information, and proxy, and list of credit cards, auto debits and payments, and user names and passwords. All updated." Then he would exclaim, "Now, let's party!" May you, too, give your family such a gift.

Unless yours is a sudden and unexpected death, someone will be called upon to make these decisions. If it isn't you, then it could be a hospital, your insurer, or a court. Or it could tear apart your family when different members hold different viewpoints.

How do you want to die? Do you want invasive procedures or not? When you know you are dying, how do you wish to spend the remaining time? With whom? Doing what?

Consider the kind of death you wish rather than specific treatments or procedures to pursue or avoid. Medical treatments may change. Your health may change. Your circumstances may change. But overarching everything is what you value for yourself. Complete these forms to record your decisions.

These are critical documents (plus your Will) to complete, update as needed, and have readily accessible. Good news: If your loved one is still of sound mind and alert, make time now to complete or update documents, as needed.

- Health Care Proxy: If you are the named primary proxy, then you are the legal decisionmaker when your loved one can no longer make health care decisions. It is best to be the sole proxy and not share this responsibility with a second party. Decisions cannot be made when persons disagree and argue over choices.

Why a proxy is important: HIPAA (the Health Insurance Portability and Accountability Act) gives everyone age 18 and older a legal right to privacy in their medical information and health records. If you are not the named proxy, you may not have the right to know about or participate in care and treatment conversations and decisions. If there is no named proxy, it may be medical personnel, insurers, or courts that make the decisions, which may disagree with what the patient would want.

Find health care proxy forms for your state at https://www. nhpco.org/patients-and-caregivers/advance-care-planning/. The names of the forms differ by state, sometimes called health care proxy, advanced care directive, or health care proxy and living will.

- Advanced Directives: These are *written, legal instructions* regarding your preferences for medical care if you are unable to make decisions for yourself. Sometimes called a living will or medical power of attorney, you indicate in writing the type of medical care desired as well as what is not wanted. (If *The Five Wishes*, a booklet offered by Hospice, is completed, then non-medical wishes, such as playing or singing favorite songs, choice of burial or cremation, and details of a memorial service, are also known.)

Why directives are important: If you have not been told how another desires to live the remaining months or days, you won't know, and you will be forced to guess when asked to make medical decisions. Furthermore, if these choices are not written down, you cannot reply with certainty to someone who is challenging your decisions.

Find your state's directives at https://www.aarp.org/caregiving/financial-legal/free-printable-advance-directives/

- POLST (Provider Orders for Life-Sustaining Treatment) form: This is a medical order which indicates the treatments you do and do not choose to accept. These choices are to be honored by all health care workers during a medical crisis.

Why this form is important: Having completed the form with your physician, your medical choices become part of your official medical record. The information should be readily accessible to all medical personnel who are involved in your care and treatment.

Obtain a form from and must be signed by your health care professional and you. Go to https://polst.org/programs-in-your-state/ to learn whether your state is part of the national POLST program.

- DNR (Do Not Resuscitate) order: tells emergency medical personnel and other medical providers whether or not to administer cardiopulmonary resuscitation (CPR).

Why a DNR is important: Emergency personnel will work to revive someone who has died, unless a DNR is in place. The physical act of resuscitation itself can break fragile ribs, complicating an otherwise serious situation. A DNR order asks you to consider whether, when natural death has occurred, you allow the letting go or wish emergency personnel to do everything possible to resuscitate the person.

A DNR order is available from your physician, hospital, or health care facility. The order is completed with a physician who must sign the form. Some states also require witnesses to sign. Free state forms are found at https://eforms.com/dnr/.

No guarantees

Although legal forms by themselves will not guarantee a drama-free, easy death, it is far better to complete and sign them. The act itself of gathering the documents offers you the opportunity to open conversations about death and dying and your current vision for your end-of-life care. Talk with and give copies to your proxy, your family, and your physicians. Explain your position so they understand your views. If you change your mind about any aspect of care, update the forms and revisit the conversations.

If you do not have these documents, you may obtain them from the above-referenced sources, others of your choosing, or your attorney.

Funeral, memorial service, and burial checklist

Personalize your memorial and burial as much as you'd like. Just as each of us has our own vision of our dying, we have our own vision of the celebration of our life and of putting that life to rest. Use this general checklist to get started.

Notifications of your death

o   A list of whom to notify—and their contact information

o   Type of announcement or message to send—which you may have already written

o   Obituary—which you may have already written

o   Letters you wrote or gifts to be delivered upon your death

How you want your life to be remembered

o   Do you want a service, gathering, or celebration while you are alive?

o   Do you want a funeral or memorial service, or both, upon your death?

▪   For a conventional funeral, contact a funeral home for arrangements, products and services

▪   Visitation or not? Open or closed casket, if used; or cremains present

- Funeral at home? https://www.youtube.com/watch?v=61F6HeAk7Ko&feature=youtu.be&list=PLUlI-RFP70hUiwtMFDkWp3c8_KuItggn6
  o A service? Where? At home, at the funeral home, at graveside, at church, at chapel, at the crematory if cremated, at another venue?
  o If there is a service:
    - Who is invited?
    - Choose readings, music
    - Speakers? Pallbearers? Other participants?
    - Flowers, decorations, photos, etc.
    - Will you record a message (audio or video) to be played at your service?
  o Request for donations? If yes, to which group(s)?
  o A marker or physical reminder of you? What? Where?

Handling of your body

  o Organ, body, or tissue donation? Make arrangements and receive permissions now
  o Burial or cremation
    - Special clothes to wear
    - Ceremony or not
    - Anything to go with you
  o If burial, where and what kind?
    - Does your family have a plot or do you need to purchase one?

- Conventional cemetery: Contact the cemetery for burial requirements and arrangements
- On own land, public hybrid burial ground or green burial ground, in land belonging to The Land Institute or similar environmental groups, park land that permits such
- Green burials
  - No embalming
  - Degradable container
o If cremation
- Conventional cremation
- Flameless, green cremation
- What will happen with the cremains?
  - Burial or scatter? Where?
o How/who will pay for the arrangements, whichever are chosen?
- Consider pre-payment in whole or in part

RESOURCES

I've confined this list to a few national groups. Search in your area for local resources.

Burial and cremation
Green Burial Council: eco-friendly end-of-life options at www.greenburialcouncil.org/ in the United States and at http://www.greenburialcanada.ca/ in Canada.

Bontz, Scott. "Rest in Perennials." *The Land Institute Land Report*, Spring 2020, pp. 4–9. www.Landinstitute.org/learn/land-report.

Flameless, green cremation: https://naturallysavvy.com/live/green-flameless-cremation/.

Caregiving and caregiver support
Caring.com: Caregiving resource center at https://www.caring.com/caregivers/.

Daily Caring: information on 11 caregiver private support groups (or search on Facebook and identify additional groups): https://dailycaring.com/support-groups-for-caregivers-on-facebook/.

Family Caregiver Alliance, National Center on Caregiving: www.caregiver.org.

National Institute on Aging—providing care and comfort at end of life: https://www.nia.nih.gov/health/providing-comfort-end-life#practical.

Complementary therapies

Benefits of acupuncture (well documented, acupuncture relieves constipation, nausea, vomiting), massage, music therapy, guided imagery, and other complementary therapies at end of life: https://www.chicagotribune.com/lifestyles/ct-xpm-2013-03-27-sc-health-0327-dying-complimentary-therapies-in-th-20130327-story.html.

Integrative Medicine and its benefits: https://nccih.nih.gov/health/integrative-health.

Death and dying support

A Good Death Foundation: www.agooddeathfoundation.com.

Death and Disability. Catapult Magazine. "An Unquiet Mind," a monthly column by s.e. smith that explores disability identity

and its interaction with the world at large. https://catapult.co/
stories/how-disability-helps-me-find-life-in-death.

National Council on Independent Living: www.ncil.org for
disability rights advocacy.

End of life Doulas, Programs and Certification, University of
Vermont Larner College of Medicine: www.Learn.uvm.edu.

International End-of-Life Doula Association (INELDA)
www.inelda.org.

Everplans.com. Guides state by state at https://www.everplans.
com/guides/state-by-state-guides.

Hospice. The Hospice Foundation of America: www.
hospicefoundation.org or the HG Foundation at www.
hospicegiving.org/.

National Hospice and Palliative Care Organization: https://
www.nhpco.org/ re advanced care directives, hospice care, grief
and bereavement, videos, and other resources.

The National Institute for Jewish Hospice: www.nijh.org.

LGBTQ support—united families and allies with the LGBTQ
community: www.pflag.org.

GLSEN (Gay Lesbian Straight Education Network): www.
glsen.org to end discrimination and bullying, and to prompt
awareness in K–12 schools.

National Center for Transgender Equality: www.transequality.org.

Grief and bereavement support

Center for Loss and Life Transition, founded by Dr. Alan Wolfelt, death educator and grief counselor: https://www. centerforloss.com/.

The Forever Family Foundation addresses grief, bereavement, afterlife: www.foreverfamilyfoundation.org.

www.thegrieftoolbox.com
www.whatsyourgrief.com

Music (bedside singing and singers)

As this ancient practice spreads, new bedside singing chapters form. Unfortunately, there is no central database at this time. In addition, current public health restrictions on visitations may affect availability. Check conditions in your local area.

To find singers or to learn more:
- https://hallowell-singers.org/services/other-hospice-choirs/ (primarily northeast U.S.; does include some choirs not listed elsewhere)

- https://thresholdchoir.org/general-content/chapters-region (choirs affiliated with Threshold Choir International)

- Call local hospice or health care facilities and ask whether they know of singers or instrumentalists

- Begin a new group—whether it is you alone, you and a friend, or a few more singers.

Can't find what you're looking for?

Contact the author at www.thecouragetocare.com.

RECOMMENDED READING

There are numerous books about death and dying. This selection, from books I've read, offers you material for divergent explorations.

Alexander, Eben, MD. *Proof of Heaven: A Neurosurgeon's Journey into the Afterlife*. New York: Simon & Schuster, 2012. The author tells of his near-death experience and what he learns.

Arnold, Johann Christoph. *Be Not Afraid: Overcoming the Fear of Death*. New York: The Plough Publishing House, 2002. Anecdotes from well-known personalities, e.g., Mother Teresa, Henri Nouwen, and others; plus stories of ordinary men, women, and children who conquer their deepest fears.

————. *Rich in Years: Finding Peace and Purpose in a Long Life*. New York: The Plough Publishing House, 2013. As a pastoral counselor focusing on aging with grace, Arnold asks spiritual and inspirational leaders the question: Why shouldn't growing older be rewarding?

Arnoldy, Francesca Lynn. *Cultivating the Doula Heart: Essentials of Compassionate Care.* Self-published. 2018. contemplativedoula. com. How to support those facing hardship, grief, and loss.

Aronson, Louise. *Elderhood: Redefining Aging, Transforming Medicine, Reimagining Life.* New York: Bloomsbury Publishing, 2019. Aronson is a geriatrician using personal and professional narratives to critique our anti-aging culture, the medical mistreatment of the old, and the pain of aging. She outlines a future where we all can age well across our lifespan.

Bernhard, Toni. *How to be Sick: A Buddhist-Inspired Guide for the Chronically Ill and their Caregivers.* Somerville, Mass.: Wisdom Publications, 2018. The author gets sick, stays that way, and shares her practices and insights on how to live joyfully and contentedly with ongoing limitations.

Bertman, Sandra L., PhD. *Facing Death—Images, Insights, and Interventions: A Handbook for Educators, Healthcare Professionals, and Counselors.* Bristol, Penn.: Taylor & Francis, 1991. Uses materials from the visual arts, poetry, fiction, drama, and popular culture to sensitize us to issues confronting both the dying and their caregivers.

Brown, Erica. *Happier Endings: A Meditation on Life and Death.* New York: Simon & Schuster, 2013. Helps you prepare for and accept death, drawing from many spiritual traditions. Stories offer surprising and poignant ways families deal with the death of a loved one.

Browne, Sylvia. *Blessings from the Other Side: Wisdom and Comfort from the Afterlife for this Life.* New York: Dutton, 2000.

———. *The Other Side and Back: A Psychic's Guide to Our World and Beyond.* New York: Signet, 2000. These are two of Browne's books which made her a number-one *New York Times* bestselling author. She was described as a psychic, medium, clairvoyant and channel with unique gifts. True stories to confirm or make you wonder.

Bryne, David. *How Music Works.* San Francisco: McSweeney's, 2012. A comprehensive tome about music, to delve deep.

Butler, Katy. *The Art of Dying Well: A Practical Guide to a Good End of Life.* New York: Scribner, 2019. How to live as well as possible for as long as possible, and adapt to health challenges. Includes insights and true stories.

———. *Knocking on Heaven's Door: The Path to a Better Way of Death.* New York: Scribner, 2013. A blend of memoir and investigative reporting about what might constitute a "good death" and the forces that stand in the way of our achieving it.

Byock, Ira, MD. *The Best Care Possible: A Physician's Quest to Transform Care through the End of Life.* New York: Avery, 2012. Byock argues that how we die represents a national crisis today. He examines medicine and ethics through real-life medical stories.

————. *Dying Well: Peace and Possibilities at the End of Life.* New York: Riverhead Books, 1997. A respected voice in the field. How to make dying conscious and peaceful.

————. *The Four Things that Matter Most: A Book About Living.* New York: Free Press, 2004. Byock explores four simple phrases—"Please forgive me," "I forgive you," "Thank you," and "I love you" (sounds like *Ho'oponopono*, doesn't it?)—and how using them regularly offers a better life and a better death.

Callanan, Maggie and Kelley, Patricia. *Final Gifts: Understanding the Special Awareness, Needs, and Communications of the Dying.* New York: Simon & Schuster, 1992. Written by hospice nurses who share true stories to inform us what to listen to and what to look for as someone dies.

Cathcart, Thomas and Klein, Daniel. *Heidegger and a Hippo Walk Through those Pearly Gates: Using Philosophy (and Jokes!) to Explore Life, Death, the Afterlife, and Everything in Between.* New York: Viking, 2009. Death isn't all doom and gloom.

Church, W.H. *Edgar Cayce's Story of the SOUL: Trace the Fascinating Footsteps of Your Evolving Soul from its Origins to its Destination.* Virginia Beach: A.R.E. Press, 1989. As a child, Cayce read the Bible all the way through in one year. Then he read more chapters each day, determined to catch up and read the Bible through as many times as his years of age. Shortly thereafter and despite little formal education, he was gifted with being able to place himself in a trance, and capable of diagnosing illnesses beyond the knowledge of contemporary physicians—often for people thousands of miles away. Given Cayce's medical accuracy—physicians took the steps Cayce recommended and patients were healed—Cayce, while in a trance state, was also asked all sorts of biblical, health, and life questions. He predicted the discovery of the Dead Sea Scrolls, and the laser. Various authors over the years collated the information by topic and published the messages. Cayce led Bible study sessions, too. Today, study groups continue to delve into the readings. Cayce continued to read the Bible through each year. Dying in 1945 at age 67, he had read the entire Bible 67 times. Cayce's A.R.E. (Association for Research and Enlightenment) preserves his more than 14,000 readings and the more than 100,000 pages of transcribed information. Visit www.edgarcayce.org and https://www.edgarcayce.org/about-us/blog/blog-posts/edgar-cayces-story-of-the-bible/.

Craven, Margaret. *I Heard the Owl Call My Name*. New York: Laurel Press, 1980. A young vicar, unaware of his terminal diagnosis, is sent to an ancient village in the Pacific Northwest. His journey of discovery teaches him—and can teach us—about life, death, and the transformative power of love. I periodically re-read this stirring short story.

Cunningham, Frank J. *Vesper Time: The Spiritual Practice of Growing Older*. Maryknoll, N.Y.: Orbis Books, 2017. Viewing aging from a spiritual perspective.

DeLeo, Kirsten. *Present through the End: A Caring Companion's Guide for Accompanying the Dying*. Boulder, Colo.: Shambhala, 2019.

Fenwick, Peter and Fenwick, Elizabeth. *The Art of Dying*. New York: Continuum, 2008. Compilation and examination of true occurrences as death nears.

Fersko-Weiss, Henry. *Caring for the Dying: The Doula Approach to a Meaningful Death*. Newburyport, Mass.: Conari Press, 2017.

Gawande, Atul, MD. *Being Mortal: Medicine and What Matters in the End*. New York: Macmillan, 2014. A new classic. Gawande argues how and why no one should die alone.

Giffels, David. *Furnishing Eternity: A Father, a Son, a Coffin, and a Measure of Life*. New York: Scribner, 2018. Reflections on life and death as father and son together plan and build the father's coffin.

Glenn, Amy Wright. *Holding Space: On Loving, Dying and Letting Go*. Berkeley, Calif.: Parallax Press, 2017. Part memoir and part spiritual reflection, Wright uses stories from her life as a hospital chaplain and asks: What does it mean to love, die, and let go?

Gordon, Steve and Kacandes, Irene. *Let's Talk About Death: Asking the Questions that Profoundly Change the Way we Live and Die*. New York: Prometheus Books, 2015. The coauthors share their several-years-long email discussion on a range of challenging questions about pain, caregiving, grief, and what comes after death. Gordon founded The Hand to Heart Project, offering in-home massage for advanced cancer patients. Kacandes is a university professor grieving after the murder of two close friends.

Gruman, Jessie. *AfterShock: What to Do When the Doctor Gives You—or Someone You Love—a Devastating Diagnosis.* New York: Walker & Co., 2007. Practical steps to assess medical options and end-of-life planning.

Guggenheim, Bill and Guggenheim, Judy. *Hello from Heaven! A new field of research—After-Death Communication—confirms that life and love are eternal.* New York: Bantam Books, 1995. True stories of connection and communication between the dead and the living.

Halifax, Joan. *Being with Dying: Cultivating Compassion and Fearlessness in the Presence of Death.* Boulder, Colo.: Shambhala, 2008. Drawing on years of caring for and training others to care for the dying, Halifax offers lessons on facing death.

Halpern, Susan P. *The Etiquette of Illness: What to Say When You Can't Find the Words.* New York: Bloomsbury, 2004. A collection of anecdotes and insights for the ill and for their families and friends, to help them say what they need.

Hanh, Thich Nhat. *No death, No fear: Comforting Wisdom for Life.* New York: Riverhead Books, 2002. A Buddhist perspective on life and death that diminishes fear.

Harper, Lynn Casteel. *On Vanishing: Mortality, Dementia, and What It Means to Disappear.* New York: Catapult, 2020. A Baptist minister's experiences lead her to question the stigma, terminology, and deficiencies of health care for persons with dementia—reminding us "vanishing is still life."

Hebb, Michael. *Let's Talk about Death (over Dinner): An Invitation and Guide to Life's Most Important Conversation.* Boston: DaCapo Lifelong Books, 2018. Practical advice for talking with your loved ones, by the founder of the death-over-dinner movement.

Holland, John. *Bridging Two Realms: Learn to Communicate with your Loved Ones on the Other Side.* Carlsbad, Calif.: Hay House, 2018. Holland is a well-known medium who shares true stories of communicating for the living with their deceased family members.

Hope, Lori. *Help Me Live: 20 things people with cancer want you to know.* Berkeley, Calif.: Celestial Arts, 2005. What helped and hurt the author during her illness. Readers, take heed.

John, Thomas. *Never Argue with a Dead Person: True and Unbelievable Stories from the Other Side.* Charlottesville, Va.: Hampton Roads, 2015. The author is a well-known medium who shares true stories corroborated by the dead's living relatives.

Johnson, Plum. *They Left us Everything: A Memoir.* New York: GP Putnam's Sons, 2014. When the author's parents avoided dealing with their possessions before they died and left it all for her, this is what she faced—and felt.

Kortes-Miller, Kathy, MD. *Talking About Death Won't Kill You: The Essential Guide to End-of-Life Conversations.* Toronto: ECW Press, 2018. Directed to Canadians, yet has practical content for everyone—from advanced care planning to talking with children, managing family dynamics, building a compassionate workplace, and more.

Kübler-Ross, Elisabeth, MD. *On Death and Dying: What the Dying Have to Teach Doctors, Nurses, Clergy and their Own Families.* New York: Scribner, 1969. A classic in the field. Kübler-Ross, who pioneered studies of and discussions with terminally ill patients about their needs and challenges, introduces and explains the five emotions commonly experienced by persons who are grieving.

Langshur, Eric and Sharon with Mary Beth Sammons. *We Carry Each Other: Getting Through Life's Toughest Times.* Berkeley, Calif.: Conari Press, 2007. How to deal with grief and loss.

Leo, Kathy. *On the Breath of Song: The Practice of Bedside Singing for the Dying.* Self-published, 2016. Founder of a New Hampshire hospice choir, Leo writes about her bedside singing experiences. www.Hallowell-singers.org.

Levine, Stephen and Levine, Ondrea. *Who Dies? An Investigation of Conscious Living and Conscious Dying.* New York: Anchor, 1989. This book inspired four of my bedside songs. Based on decades of providing emotional and spiritual support for the dying, the authors believe that participating fully in living is the best preparation for whatever comes next.

MacLeod, Ainslie. *The Instruction: Living the Life Your Soul Intended.* Boulder, Colo.: Sounds True, 2009. For you who are open to exploring how the spiritual and physical planes are connected and the mystery of who you are and why you're here.

McVea, Crystal. *Chasing Heaven: What Dying Taught Me About Living*. Brentwood, Tenn.: Howard Books, 2016. The author's near-death-experience story and lessons learned.

Miller, B.J., MD and Berger, Shoshana. *A Beginner's Guide to the End: Practical Advice for Living Life and Facing Death*. New York: Simon & Schuster, 2019. An action plan for control in freeing up as much time as possible to live until death.

Moll, Rob. *The Art of Dying: Living Fully into the Life to Come*. Downer's Grove, Ill.: IVP Books, 2010. Based on interviews with medical professionals, families, and spiritual counselors, this guide for Christians tells how to live well and prepare for death.

Moody, Raymond, MD. *Life after Life*. New York: Bantam Books, 1975. The *New York Times* calls Dr. Moody "the father of the near-death experience." A classic in the field. Exploration of near-death experiences—their prevalence, descriptions, and similarities.

Morris, Virginia. *Talking about Death*. Chapel Hill, N.C.: Algonquin Books, 2004. Addresses the cultural, personal, medical, and legal concerns that are necessary for us—as individuals and as a society—to prepare for a good death.

Nepo, Mark. *The Book of Awakening: Having the Life You Want by Being Present to the Life You Have*. Berkeley, Calif.: Conari

Press, 2000. Offers a short reflection plus a brief meditation for each day.

Nuland, Sherwin B. *How We Die: Reflections on Life's Final Chapter.* New York: Alfred A. Knopf, 1994. A classic in the field.

O'Donohue, John. *Anam Cara: A Book of Celtic Wisdom.* San Francisco: Harper Perennial, 1998. Gaelic for "soul friend," *Anam Cara* offers insights on friendship, solitude, love, and death.

Oliver, Mary. *House of Light: Poems.* Boston: Beacon Press, 1990. Oliver won a Pulitzer prize for her poetry.

————. *What Do We Know: Poems and prose poems.* Boston: DaCapo Press, 2002. Take delight in Oliver's poetic imagery of life and of death.

Pogrebin, Letty Cottin. *How to be a Friend to a Friend Who's Sick.* New York: Public Affairs. 2013. Recounting her cancer journey as well as sharing advice from patients and others with serious illness, the author tells how best to comfort, help, and simply talk to someone who is sick.

Rinpoche, Songal. *The Tibetan Book of Living and Dying.* San Francisco: Harper One, 2002. A comforting manual with practices and meditations for life and death, introducing Tibetan Buddhist wisdom. An international spiritual classic.

Sacks, Oliver. *Gratitude.* New York: Knopf, 2015. During the last months of his life, Sacks wrote a set of essays exploring his feelings about completing a life and coming to terms with his own death. His predominant feeling was gratitude for the gift of life.

Speerstra, Karen and Anderson, Herbert. *The Divine Art of Dying: How to Live Well While Dying.* Studio City, Calif.: Divine Arts, 2014. Combining personal stories with research on palliative and hospice care, the authors look at the spiritual dimensions of living fully when death is near.

Thoreau, Henry David. *Letters to a Spiritual Seeker.* New York: W.W. Norton & Co., 2004. An exchange of letters in which Thoreau offers views on spirituality.

Tisdale, Sallie. *Advice for Future Corpses (And Those Who Love Them): A Practical Perspective on Death and Dying.* New York: Touchstone, 2018. A former palliative care nurse, Tisdale looks at communication, good deaths, the dying process, handling of the body, and grief.

Trott, Susan. *The Holy Man.* New York: Riverhead Books, 1995.

———. *The Holy Man's Journey.* New York: Riverhead Books, 1997. Both of these books of fiction by Trott offer thoughtful perspectives about life's journey. Aren't we each holy?

Van Praagh, James. *Ghosts Among Us: Uncovering the Truth About the Other Side.* San Francisco: Harper One, 2008. Van Praagh is a well-known medium. True stories from his experiences.

Walsch, Neale Donald. *Home with God in a Life that Never Ends.* New York: Atria Books, 2006. This is the last book in

Walsch's *Conversations with God* series, exploring existence and transcendence.

Walters, Kerry. *The Art of Dying and Living: Lessons from Saints of Our Time.* Maryknoll, N.Y.: Orbis Books, 2011. Recounts the lives and virtues of seven women and men of modern times.

Wanzer, Sidney, MD and Glenmullen, Joseph, MD. *To Die Well: Your Right to Comfort, Calm, and Choice in the Last Days of Life.* Philadelphia: DaCapo Press, 2007. A guide by two doctors detailing end-of-life options including the right to refuse treatment, insist on pain medication, receive honest information from physicians, control dying, and pass with dignity.

Watson, Linda. *Facing Death: A companion in words and images.* Baltimore: Health Professions Press, 2009. Photographs and brief passages for use in quiet contemplation.

Wehr, Janet, RN. *Peaceful Passages: A Hospice Nurse's Stories of Dying Well.* Wheaton, Ill.: Quest Books, 2015. Used as a training manual by Hospice of America, offers true stories of achieving peaceful, even joyful, dying. Includes assessment of hospice services.

Wrenn, Paula and Gustely, Jo, RN, BSN, CHPN. *Dying Well with Hospice: A Compassionate Guide to End of Life Care.* San Diego, Calif.: Amans Vitae Press, 2017. Explains starting conversations and advanced planning for the dying process and hospice services.

ACKNOWLEDGMENTS

For several years, I considered writing an account of my experiences with death and dying. I saw too many people, alone, as they moved toward death. One day, my cousin Bill took me aside and said, "You're good at this. If you haven't thought of making it your life's work, you should." I realized then that I was passionate about journeying with the dying as they neared their last breath. And I saw the need for others to serve in this way. Dr. Elisabeth Kübler-Ross' early influence, the more recent writings of Dr. Atul Gawande, and others, as well as my bedside singing and hospice vigil experiences, spurred me to begin—long before this pandemic.

While writing, I became aware of a professional certificate End-of-Life Doula program through the University of Vermont Larner College of Medicine. Confirmed in my knowledge as well as introduced to new perspectives, the approach and content of the program—developed and facilitated by Program Director Francesca Lynn Arnoldy—enriched my understanding, and benefits those whom I joyfully serve.

Decades ago and in another state, I met Windy Woodland, who opened up the world of meditation, spiritual healing, and rose readings. My formation as a Spiritualist minister through the ordination program at Fellowships of the Spirit was the capstone, solidifying my knowing of a continuing life after the event that is called death. From this perspective—and with additional experiences since—I feel comfortable with death and dying, having befriended this part of life and living. It is no wonder I now do what I do.

I continue to be in awe of the power of music at the bedside. Profound in their simplicity, Threshold songs touch our deepest places. Sincere appreciation to Maria Culberson, Melanie DeMore, Irene Favreau, Terry Garthwaite, Patricia Hallam, Kate Munger, Becky Reardon, Patricia McKernon Runkle, Penelope Salinger, Kate Schuyler, and Marilyn Power Scott—who gave permission to share excerpts from their songs. These songwriters and many more have contributed to the repertoire of Threshold Choir International (TCI), of which I am a member. Please refer to the Sources and Notes section for fuller information about their songs.

I wish to recognize Kate Munger, who founded TCI so many years ago, and Carol Emanuel, who introduced me to the idea and practice of bedside singing. The vision continues to unfold as the pandemic restrictions interrupt our bedside presence. For all bedside singers who are committed to this ministry, freely giving their time and talent to be companions—fully present—to the dying, including the Berkshire Threshold Choir and especially Michelle Kuzia, who was my devoted singing partner, thank you all from the bottom of my heart.

Stories are the threads that give color to a narrative. Much gratitude and love to the Amann Family, Leslie Bridger, David Bryce, the Cannon-Dornell Family, Kevin Conklin, Rosie Guagliardo, Stephanie Hale, Kymn Harvin, Christine Kloser, David Kloser, Judith Melevage, Carole Moreland, Gary Niki, Kim Parry and Jamie Zimron who shared theirs. May our readers be enriched by the telling.

To Sharon, Michelle, and especially to Malcolm for your early reading of *The Courage to Care*. Your careful reading and insights made this a better book.

For the enthusiastic support and encouragement of my fellow authors and the entire team of Christine Kloser's Breakthrough! and Accelerator Get Your Book Done programs, hugs and blessings. It has been a joy to be part of the Transformational Author Community. You sustained my Going into the Roar!

We each, at any moment, are the culmination of our life's experiences to that point. Here I stand, today, formed by so many people, writers, workshops, retreats, programs, and songs too numerous to mention and beyond my recollection, but these persons must not be forgotten. For Lloyd Short of blessed memory, devoted father and husband, and for our extraordinary children, Rebecca, Kathleen, Elisabeth, and Michael, you all are and will remain a glorious part of me. And for dear David who today and always wants only for me to grow into the best of who I am. You are a precious gift.

CONTACT
LINDA BRYCE

ADDRESS:
20 Prospect Lake Road
Great Barrington, MA 01230

PHONE:
(413) 717-9910

MAIN WEBSITE:
www.thecouragetocare.com

- For speaking engagements, quantity discounts, promotions of *The Courage to Care: How to be Fully Present with the Dying;*
- For prints of *One Person can Make a Difference* and *Go Into the Roar* and related items;

- For further information, or to make comments or to ask questions, contact Linda directly.
- Want to share your story of an experience you had with someone dying? Please email me! I look forward to hearing from you.

EMAIL:
Linda@thecouragetocare.com

FOLLOW LINDA ONLINE:
www.thecouragetocare.com
www.thecouragetocare.com/blog

FOLLOW LINDA ON SOCIAL MEDIA:
www.linkedin.com/in/linda-bryce-m-a-rev-6492671b6/
www.facebook.com/linda.bryce.94651
www.instagram.com/lindabryce48/

ABOUT THE AUTHOR

L INDA BRYCE, M.A., Rev., is an engaging educator and author. Her compassion and focus have encompassed seemingly unrelated areas of life. As a teen, she volunteered at a county hospital and helped establish a neighborhood health clinic. She then served the elderly, children, and families as an attorney through her presentations and her writings, integrating her spiritual understanding with matters of the day, including nursing home reform and planning an adult day program in her neighborhood.

Her meditation practice and spiritual healing deepened her interior life. She created and published religious education materials and study guides, authored a book on self-healing, gave workshops on personal development, and eventually returned to graduate school to earn a Master's degree in Jewish–Christian Studies. She joined the faculty of The Pennsylvania State University to teach in the Religious Studies, Jewish Studies, and History Departments, and became an ordained Spiritualist minister.

Life changes, particularly the death of her husband, led Linda to the bedside—becoming a bedside singer and writer of songs for the dying, a hospice vigil volunteer, and a recipient of a professional certificate as an end-of-life doula.

Remarried and living in the Berkshires of western Massachusetts, Linda enjoys exploring new outdoor places. Her fondest memories are of her hikes into Machu Picchu on the Camino Inca, and her solo 130-mile trek on the coastal path around the Isle of Anglesey, Wales, during which she wrote *Be at Peace,* an often-sung favorite.